THE INGREDIENTS FOR BUILDING YOUR DREAM

Creative Leadership
Physical Asset Management
Asset Management Capability and Culture

PMM Institute for Learning
Valencia, Spain

THE INGREDIENTS FOR BUILDING YOUR DREAM

Luigi Amendola, Ph.D.

ISBN 978-1-941872-53-6
HF112016

Publisher: Reliabilityweb.com

Design and Layout: Apolonia Lemus

For information: Reliabilityweb.com
www.reliabilityweb.com
8991 Daniels Center Drive, Suite 105, Ft. Myers, FL 33912
Toll Free: 888-575-1245 | Phone: 239-333-2500
E-mail: crm@reliabilityweb.com

Printed in Spain
Legal depository: V-1240-2015

ISBN: 978-1-941872-53-6
Printed by Coprint.com

---

10 9 8 7 6 5 4 3 2 1

"Making each day a mini lifetime – to achieve something and to enjoy something."

Joan Collins

Renowned actress from the Dynasty television series

"Brands are no longer competing against each other, they are competing against speed."

Marc Benioff

Chairman and CEO of Salesforce

"But in the end, what's your secret for being on top for 30 years? Being humble, asking lots of questions, being on the streets and doing things as best possible."

Juan Mari Arzak

Award-winning chef and restaurant owner in Spain

ACKNOWLEDGMENTS

Once you finish strenuous work filled with difficulties – like the development of a book on asset management – it's inevitable to be taken over by a very human egocentrism that leads you to focus most of its merit on your own contribution. However, objective analysis immediately shows that the magnitude of that contribution would have been impossible without the participation of the PMM Institute for Learning team. I thank them for easing things along, allowing this work to come to a happy ending.

My fundamental acknowledgment goes to those who live all the processes in my life: my family, my teachers and my colleagues, all of whom always patiently understand and respect my immersion in books for hours, leaving other pleasures, like dining on Sundays or Friday afternoon beers, for later. To them, my infinite thanks for their understanding and support.

To all those entrepreneurs who fundamentally taught me that dreams with actions are productive realities.

To my clients, who each day allow me to work to strengthen their organizations.

To all of you who spend time reading these ideas to construct your dreams. Many thanks for being there and welcome to thinking about ASSET MANAGEMENT.

To the Holiest Mother of the Valley, Luigi (my father) and Iginia (my mother), my most profound acknowledgment for all the favors you have conceded to this day. You were and are the Road, Truth and Life.

Great things in businesses are never done by one person alone; they are always done by a group.

We don't always have the opportunity to do many things, that's why each thing we do should be excellent.

Luigi Amendola, PhD
CEO & Managing Director
PMM Institute for Learning
Director PMM Business School

MENU

Suggested menu
by Chef

Aperitifs

Introduction

Many of you have probably asked the same questions about dreams: What are dreams? What do the messages from destiny mean? Why do memories from my past tell me? What do these feelings, experiences, traumas, jealousies put away in my subconscious mean? What is the literal or symbolic development of truth? Or is it the result of neurological problems?

For asset management, dreams are ideas that, when constructed, become opportunities. How many of you have dreamt with your eyes open? How many ideas come up from conversations with coworkers, at home with the kids, or simply chatting over food or after the meal? How many of those dreams turn into disappointing sighs because you haven't constructed them into solid plans, put together an appropriate team, or simply don't believe these dreams represent value to anybody?

"The Ingredients for Building Your Dream" is a joint project with my collaborators, where we have put all our efforts and hopes in trying to engage asset managers and appeal to their most creative side, always searching for company developments that will take them to the top. In this book, I talk about life experiences I have had throughout my career in industry and academia, executing all the roles in physical asset management, including mechanic technician, instrumentalist, supervisor, superintendent, operations and maintenance manager, and general manager.

This book is a big goal and I hope to have such an ambitious project take off, where talent and imagination come together to make asset management a pleasure for the senses. From my love of good food, the intercultural synergy that runs in my veins and the long conversations after meals, I propose a new approach to the enjoyment of dreaming, imagining and creating. This approach brings together two of my most profound passions: asset management and good eating. What's yours?

Building your dream in a company or organization is like a type of dream in which you appear to be awake and act, move, go back and forth as automatons along the same paths and in the same way. It's like the racehorse with blinders that can only look ahead.

People appear to be asleep in a parallel world we call reality and it's in this reality where it's often unclear how to build your dreams and finally make them real. The construction of your dream in asset management is akin to fixing your eyes on a point in the horizon to guide your objectives, policies and strategic plans. It's like that something that appears superior and sublime, but is the success that people say they want. So, building your dreams is waking up from that dream in which the environment has you – competition in asset management, economic profit, social status, personal acceptance – and conditions your decisions to large or small measures.

Dreaming for the implementation of asset management in your company means the company can achieve sustainability of its business. With this approach, it will experiment with positive changes in the tangible, intangible, financial and non-financial realms, as specified by the International Organization for Standardization (ISO) in ISO 55001 for asset management (AM).

Organizations that have implemented asset management represent references in the economic, social and environmental realms, and dreaming along that path means you are ready to join them. If you dream of having an excellent organization, that means current ambitions are in your dreams. An immediate step is to begin constructing your dreams to reach that much dreamed of state of operational excellence.

So, if building your dreams implies achieving happiness, then what is happiness? Stop for a moment, sit down, close your eyes, put your left hand on your heart and ask yourself: What makes me happy? Your answer could lead you to the process of making your dreams come true and that, itself, might be the REAL accomplishment of happiness in asset management.

Plan, program, execute and continuously follow-up. Write your dreams down on a daily list and work toward achieving each of them. Remember, dreams have no limits. Let them come out, don't criticize or destroy them beforehand. Wake them up at first for yourself and later search for alternatives to achieve them in your organization with your team. Share your dreams with everyone in the organization once you've advanced their realization so criticism doesn't stop you. Share your experience.

The Recipe for Constructing Asset Management

By: Tibaire Depool, PhD
Executive, PMM Institute for Learning

Given that this book is an ode to good eating, in particular to the Mediterranean menu that fosters the tradition of a starter, main dish and dessert, along with good company (teamwork), it is important to highlight how eating well fits perfectly with what happens with teams and organizations when they begin a process of implementing or optimizing physical asset management.

This chapter shows the analogy between how the keys to eating healthily is very much like the recipe for success in the implementation of physical asset management.

A healthy diet consists of foods that avoid an increase in body fat that would slow down your metabolism and lead to weight gain. In asset management, a healthy program promotes the health of your assets so they do not run slower, become weightier, or operate ineffectively or inefficiently.

Eating healthily and having healthy assets have quite a bit in common in terms of the processes to get there. Here are some examples:

In order to reach your ideal or target weight, innumerable diets or weight loss programs exist. A food diet regulates appetite. In asset management, it can be related to the evaluation of indicators.

Some diets promise weight loss in little time. In asset management, these would be short-term actions. However, these diets have demonstrated a rebound effect that results in people on them to regain initial weight or double it. The same happens when an organization wants to begin a physical asset management project. On occasion, they seek magic formulas or others, such as contract consultants, to exercise for them without the organization involved in doing the work. That, in profound agreement with my experience and that of my team, **does not work**.

Other organizations start a physical asset project with a lot of enthusiasm (as diets are frequently started), however, in the middle of the process, they lose interest and by the end, the project falls and the result is great backtracking and a loss of employed effort. In diets, it would be regaining or doubling your weight.

Other organizations manage to reach benefits starting from the implementation of an asset management system, but fail by thinking that the goal has been reached. This causes a rebound effect or backtracking to the initial phase or worse. The same occurs with diets that are poorly carried out.

On the other hand, weight loss methods exist that promote sustainability, that is, mitigating the risk of a rebound effect (or regaining lost weight in dieting). However, these diets or programs require a lot of sacrifice and discipline, which requires dieters to have support and a strong conviction that what they begin they will develop adequately and finish it.

One of the keys to success when cooking up an asset management system that is sustainable and generates value is that organizations recognize that:

- Asset management is not a 100 meter dash, but rather an ultra-marathon.
- Responsibility is not only in maintenance, but rather a coordinated activity in the whole organization.
- Asset management is not document management, nor is it only oriented toward generating a registry, given the fact that it has an International Organization for Standardization (ISO) standard, ISO 55001, behind it.

- If the best way of taking care of your body is knowing it and knowing what does it harm or not, in this sense, the best way of implementing an asset management initiative is knowing what it is for or its benefits.

Figure 1 shows the 12345 method for a new lifestyle taken as a reference from a weight loss program. This method has two phases. The first is divided into three steps that seek to define your starting weight (in asset management, diagnosis and identification of the baseline) and define ideal weight (in asset management, target or objective). The second phase is associated with weight maintenance, assuring there will be no rebound effect (in asset management, this is step back).

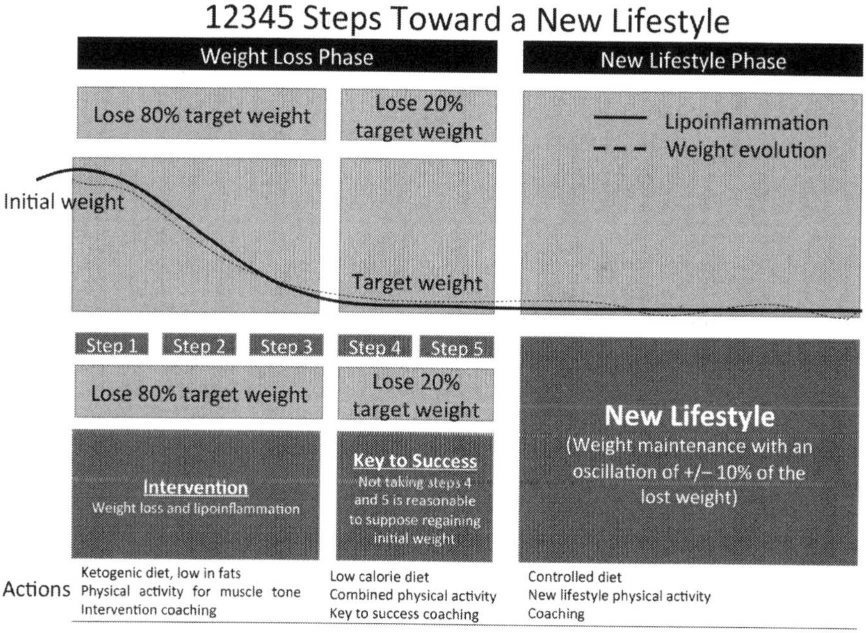

Figure 1: Scheme for weight loss and lifestyle improvement steps *(Adapted from Pronokal Method)*

In the figure, the objective of losing eighty percent of the target weight is defined in the weight loss phase, as well as the necessary actions to reach it. It's important to highlight that a constant action in all phases is coaching. Coaching is considered a key to success, assuring the dieter can reach a healthy lifestyle.

In analyzing this method, even when you begin with the weight loss goal, the end result or end goal is really to keep the target weight (generation of value through physical asset management). Therefore, by losing weight, the project is yet unfinished, that is, the end has not been reached. This implies the process continues through maintenance of new lifestyle habits. In physical asset management, once implementation has been satisfactorily achieved, one must assure good practices continue to be maintained, that the cultural change is developing adequately and a vigilance process is in place so the adequate system continues to be up-to-date.

Steps 4 and 5 in Figure 1 are oriented toward the transition phase of the gap closure stage and the stage for maintenance or the adoption of a new lifestyle. In asset management, it would be the adoption of good practices. It can be appreciated that the key to both the success of a weight loss program and an asset management program is in taking these steps, which implies that although eighty percent of the goal has been reached, not reaching the remaining twenty percent to get to one hundred percent increases the risk that there will be backtracking in the process.

In the weight loss and medical arenas, the term lipo means fat. Two definitions of lipo are equally valid and useful for the physical asset management environment.

1. Lipo – prefix that forms names and adjectives and whose meaning is "fat."
2. Lipo – prefix that forms parts of names and adjectives with the meaning "absence of."

In the asset management context, we will transform the lipo term to lipo-AM and lipoassetmanagement and define them this way.

- LIPO-AM – a consequence of doing many things, such as projects and asset-related activities, without efficacious results that generate value. On occasion, the activities and implementations that have been done produce backtracking or loss of quality or standards that tend to accumulate hidden losses and actions that are carried out without control.

- Lipoassetmanagement – the absence of physical asset management or development of actions or implementations in an isolated manner; a thinking that physical asset management is being applied, but without an integral solution.

In this sense, a recipe to achieve asset management implementation should be directed in both terms. On one hand, it must assure that physical asset management exists and develop actions to mitigate LIPOI-AM. In this sense, shortcuts don't exist, nor do magic formulas. Rather, as with a weight loss program, a structured process is needed with continual monitoring to assure that actions are having the desired effect.

The PMM Institute for Learning method for breaking with LIPO-AM and lipoassetmangement, as shown in Figure 2, features phases associated with implementation and optimization of physical asset management.

Identifying losses and evaluating the gap between how things are being done today and how they should be done is performed in the first stage. The second stage clearly defines the baseline from which progress will be evaluated. Also in this stage, two key aspects are started: technology and structure, and competencies.

Stage 3 is directed toward implementation of adequate strategies according to the baseline or road map defined.

Stages 4 and 5 address sustainability and certification, much like a weight loss model.

Stage 6 ensures the organization does not fall into inertia and continues to work toward assuring physical asset management is adequate and answers the needs of the organization.

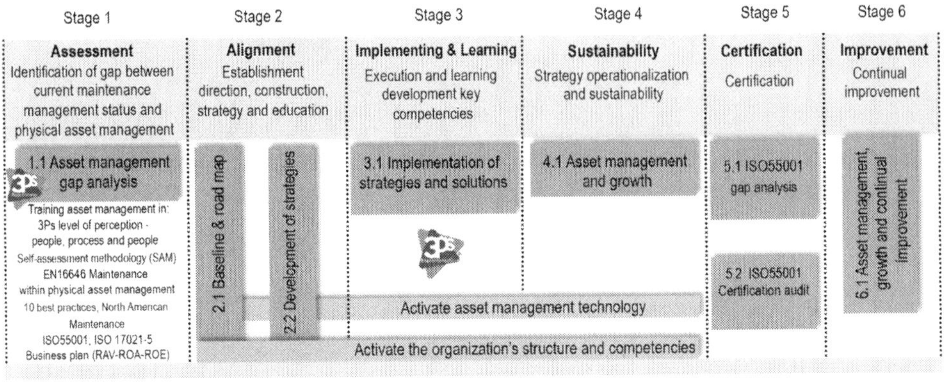

Figure 2: Implementation stages for physical asset management *(Amendola, L., Depool, T., 2011, 2014, 2016)*

In order to follow these stages, I recommend thirteen ingredients that will allow for successful implementation of physical asset management. Given that this book talks about how to achieve a balanced menu that is enjoyable to the palate, I propose the following menu:

1. One starter to prepare the stomach;
2. One main dish to be enjoyed;
3. Dessert to celebrate achievements;
4. Digestive so you don't forget that a good meal integrates us all.

Next, a recipe is provided to help you be a good host in physical asset management and, therefore, manage to have visitors stay and be your guests in the long term.

Two versions of a menu are provided, depending on how hungry you are (i.e., the extent of your organization's needs). The first version is based on the 3Ps assessment elements of the PMM Institute for Learning.

Menu 1: Maintenance Within Asset Management

All plates are harmoniously united with coaching or accompaniment and motivation.	
STARTER (LAYING THE GROUND)	
Ingredients: 1. Management strategy 2. Planning and programming 3. Performance measures 4. Employee involvement 5. Information on infrastructure and facilities	Name of the Plate: "CONSCIENCE" with pepper and apple* coulis (*) The green color of the apple makes reference to the level of conscious maturity.
MAIN DISH (CONSTRUCTING SUSTAINABILITY)	
Ingredients: 1. Organization and its people 2. Materials management 3. Maintenance techniques 4. Information technology & use 5. Process analysis 6. Process safety management	Name of the Plate: "COMPETENCY" in Roquefort* cream (*) The blue color in the cheese makes reference to the level of competent maturity.
DIGESTIVE (INTEGRATION AND SUSTAINABILITY)	
Ingredients: 1. Reliability analysis 2. Certification and recognition	Name of the Plate: "EXCELLENCE" in wine with red fruits
"CONTINUAL IMPROVEMENT" in gold champagne	

Only cooking and inviting remains!

Menu 2: Asset Management

All plates are harmoniously united with coaching or accompaniment and motivation.	
STARTER (LAYING THE GROUND)	
Ingredients: 1. Business plan 2. Alignment of operations and maintenance (O&M), enablers and business strategy 3. O&M education and physical asset enablers 4. GAP analysis 5. Road map and baseline	Name of the Plate: "CONSCIENCE" with green artichoke* from the garden and a wine reduction (*) The green color of the artichoke makes reference to the level of conscious maturity.
MAIN DISH (CONSTRUCTING SUSTAINABILITY)	
Ingredients: 1. Updating objectives and plans of the organization 2. Asset management policy 3. Strategic asset management plan 4. Asset management plans 5. Implementation of the plans (cost-benefit)	Name of the Plate: "COMPETENCY" with blue lobster* cooked in butter (*) The blue color makes reference to the level of competent maturity.
DIGESTIVE (INTEGRATION AND SUSTAINABILITY)	
Ingredients: 1. Yield evaluation of the key performance indicator (KPI) assets, both strategic and tactical 2. Certification and recognition	Name of the Plate: "EXCELLENCE" with strawberries and cream
"CONTINUAL IMPROVEMENT" in gold champagne	

HARMONIOUS UNION

All plates are harmoniously united with coaching and motivation.

If what you want is to try the delicate process of alcoholic fermentation of the grape in the form of a quality wine, our chef proposes these varieties, which, no doubt, will set the bar high.

Chef Recommended Grape Varietals:
Sauvignon, Mourvèdre and Cariñena

Let yourself be swept up by the aromas of this precious drink that accompanies any good meal that calls itself such.

A touch of hope, motivation and dreams.

Bon appetit!

Starters

LET'S TALK ABOUT HISTORY

Knowing about the past helps you understand the present and model the future.

The term asset management is not new. People have managed assets for thousands of years. However, what has changed is the current acknowledgment of optimal asset management, in which factors, such as cost, yield and risks, are combined and applied to the whole lifecycle of the asset.

Let's take a quick look at the past to see how we arrived at today.

Historical Timeline

April 1970 – British industry forms a committee focused on terotechnology to advise the government on better methods that could be employed by applying terotechological practices in the commercial and industrial life of a company.

1973 – The application of terotechnology extends throughout the world of engineering. The next step was to conduct a study of five hundred defective buildings during the period of 1970 to 1974. The study reveals that in fifty-eight percent of the sample, defects were attributable to design defects, thirty-five percent to poor execution, twelve percent to bad materials or systems and eleven percent to unforeseen requests by the user.

Norm BS3711:1974 (now BS3811:1984) was created as a result of the study, defining terotechnology as the combination of all technical and associated administrative techniques tending toward preserving an item or reestablishing it to a state so it can perform the required function. Additionally, it indicates the required function can be defined as a condition.

1990 – The industrial crisis of the 1980s drove companies to conduct big efforts in cost reduction. These cost reductions were carried out without evaluating the implicit risks, resulting in large losses in safety, production and infrastructure.

This same year, the North American Maintenance Excellence Award (NAME) was created to promote quality and competition through the definition of "good practices" of maintenance. In addition to recognizing lead companies, NAME disseminated these companies' best practices, strategies and benefits. Through this exchange of information, the ten good practices of maintenance management were defined.

Ten Good Maintenance Management Practices

1. Teamwork
2. Selection of contractors oriented toward productivity
3. Integration with materials and service providers
4. Manager's support and vision
5. Proactive planning and programming
6. Continual improvement
7. Disciplined management of the materials stock
8. Integration of systems
9. Management of plant stops
10. Production based on reliability

1993 – The Institute of Asset Management (IAM) was created, grouping diverse companies that were interested in sharing experiences and good practices. The new practices consolidate a discipline known as asset management and spur a major change in the United Kingdom, Australia and New Zealand.

1995-1998 - Important companies in Britain, Australia and New Zealand associate themselves with IAM. The need to create solid bases for asset management is established in different markets and industries.

2003 -The British Standards Institution (BSI) committee in asset management is established.

2004 - BSI's PAS55 specifications are published, complementing and supporting ISO 9001, ISO 14000 and the Occupational Health and Safety Assessment Series' OHSAS18000 standards.

2010 - The great acceptance of PAS55 leads the ISO technical committee to create an international standard for asset management. Based on the PAS55 document, the ISO 55000 suite of standards considers everything that had been done until then, but in a more systematic way.

2014 - Public presentation of the ISO 55001 standard for asset management. With the current competitiveness in businesses characterized by cuts in budgets, time pressures, high quality requirements and growing demands from consumers, coupled with the globalization of markets, environmental demands and the current financial crisis, AM policies allow organizations to optimize their technical, economic, social, organizational and human resources.

In this way, AM has become the framework of a coexistence of strategies, methodologies, norms, standards and techniques that are necessary to generate sustainable value through the optimized management of assets. As such, the close link that exists between good asset management and the achievement of strategic objectives becomes clear.

The Arrival of Asset Management

The idea of asset management arrived from three different fronts.

The first front is linked to the financial services sector, which has been employing the term for more than one hundred years to describe the act of optimization of risk of short, medium and long term yield and the safety of a mixed portfolio of cash, stocks and other investments.

The second front occurred in 1970 when England's Ministry for Public Buildings and Works and the Mercury House's Journal of Maintenance Engineering sponsored a congress on the sustainable maintenance of buildings. It was then when the decision to replace the term economy of maintenance with the term terotechnology was made. But, what is terotechnology?

Terotechnology is a concept that was incorporated within systems of industrial management. It comes from the Greek tero-tecno-logos, meaning the study and management of the life of an asset, from the costs of the original design in the concept phase, including the basic engineering, detail, construction and installation, plus the total cost of the property, including the operational and maintenance costs, to the final compensation of the life of the asset, implying the economic management of the asset. This concept can be applied to products in general, given that the final products of a company can sometimes be another's assets.

Terotechnology also applies to the management, finance, engineering and other practices applied to physical assets, such as facilities, machinery, equipment, buildings and structures in the search for the economic costs of the lifecycle. Decisions in terotechnology are influenced by design information, yield and costs throughout the lifecycle of a project. It integrates logistics, engineering, management, or company finances in a global whole from which they operate together.

Afterward, the North Sea Oil and Gas Company adopted terotechnology as its asset management term following the Piper Alpha disaster and the fall of oil prices at the end of the 1980s.

The third front occurred in Australia and New Zealand when the public sector confronted a "perfect storm" as the level of government services dropped, which brought about cost increases and poor planning in the industry. Public protest forced directors, specialists and technicians to go back and think of a new way of establishing better strategic planning. The priority was to think and improve what they convened calling "physical assets."

In these three environments, the parties involved took note of the need for change in management. In the case of the oil sector, they discovered that the creation of small and dynamic multidisciplinary teams to manage each of the oil platforms (i.e., the asset), taking into account the whole lifecycle, generated notable improvements in yield, safety and productivity.

Defining Asset Management

The message and lessons learned through the years reached sectors, including public water services, electricity, facilities, oil and gas, infrastructure and roads, train transport systems, mining, processes and the manufacturing industry, at an accelerated rate. They all realized that great opportunities are found in sustainability and optimization of the lifecycles of their physical assets.

Taking everything from the past into consideration, asset management (AM) can be defined as a group of practices and holistic coordinated activities from which an organization can manage its physical assets in an optimal way, taking into consideration aspects associated with performance, risks and management of its lifecycle. All of this is directed toward accomplishing the organization's strategic plans, as outlined in the ISO 55000 standards for asset management.

ISO 55000 defines AM as "the coordinated activity of an organization to realize value from assets" and an asset as "an item, thing, or entity that has potential or actual value to an organization."

AM can be further defined as the integral management of assets, visualizing it as a system of controls in which everything must be carefully measured and optimized. It consists, therefore, in a management of tangible and non-tangible assets, an integrated proposal to operate, maintain, improve and adapt the plants and infrastructure of an organization with the aim of creating an environment that firmly supports the strategic objectives of a company.

AM is also considered a process of reasoning; self-evaluation; developing strategies, objectives and action plans for the implementation and sustainability of the assets; and coordinating knowledge and functions of the entire organization. According to the International Infrastructure Management Manual, AM is the combination of the areas of financial, economic management, engineering and other practices applied to physical assets with the object of providing the level of service required in a profitable way.

Considering the different definitions of AM, one can conclude that it isn't exclusive to any one department or area of the company, but rather integrates all the areas of an organization in a coordinated way, focusing on generating value through assets. In doing so, the organization should be conscious of the distance between how they do it today and how they should do it according to good practices and fundamental references, such as norms, standards, guides, etc.

The correct application of the techniques for facility management allows companies to provide the adequate environment for directing the nucleus of their economic activity on the basis of cost efficiency and a good quality price relationship. AM is not focused on performing actions on assets so much as it is in generating value through these. That is, it is focused on a sustainable yield of the economic activity.

Chef's Recommendations:

There are many fundamental references, including standards, guides, international norms, European norms, Norwegian norms, American norms, etc., that facilitate the road that others have taken and are therefore useful. But, they should be used with conscience; that is, understand what you eat and in that way, you will know whether or not your palate and stomach are prepared for more sophisticated food.

With the presentation of ISO 55001, many companies believe it is only documentation, records, and process definitions and its objective is only certification. These beliefs are far from the truth.

ISO 55001 is an operational norm that guides asset-intensive companies (i.e., companies that depend on physical assets to generate wealth) to generate value by aligning assets to the business plan. Achieving certification means the company or organization has demonstrated it is generating value. This is the consequence that must be achieved with the adoption of the standard and associated practices.

PRE-CRISIS ENVIRONMENT AND CRISIS ECONOMIC CYCLES

War Without Bombs

Beyond globalization and consumerism, national economies need to function to produce goods and services, with the object of satisfying those needs. This allows job, wealth and development creation on the basis of effective resources and existing opportunities.

In a war without bombs, disorders begin to alter the conditions of industries. Some of the most important influencing factors are economic expansion, relaxation of credit, debt increases, key increases in asset value with the creation of economic bubbles, the start of a more restrictive monetary policy, a drop in asset prices and economic recession.

Crises can be categorized into three situations: industrial, monetary, or mercantile. Crises are created by obstacles that create a disequilibrium between offer and demand of products.

The effects of crises extend rapidly to economic movements and always take on the same characteristics: a shutdown of factories leave products sitting, salaries go down, investors flee from the market, credit disappears, interest rises, prices have abrupt oscillations and a lack of capital ensues. The producer suffers from all of this, the consumer from deprivation and all parties arrive at desolation and misery.

Crises create economic cycles that can serve as a platform for innovation. Economic cycles have various impacts:

- Loss of income and benefits create, at first, a cost cutting mentality, which is good for innovation.
- Quick action, since when the patient is bleeding, the first thing you have to do is stop the hemorrhaging.
- A phase in which leaders try to figure out which parts of their business model are not going well or are unsustainable.
- Restructuring and reinvention of the business begins.

A very important thing is excess of precaution or an exaggerated dependence on incremental innovation to the detriment of transforming, known as disruptive innovation. The largest gains of a company come from bold innovations that challenge paradigms and the company.

What can be done so economic cycles don't become an excuse for not investing in new strategies for asset management? What should you do to apply counterintuitive measures? And what should you do so you're not waiting for a crisis to occur, but always do the correct things or search for continuous improvement?

When confronting new challenges, even if the human mind associates economic cycles or priorities with negative aspects, look at them as an opportunity. Here are some factors to consider.

Operationalize Company Strategies

The need for companies to increase their business competitiveness and make it more dynamic will likely require an increase in investment in innovation and minimization of production expenses. At the same time, the changes in strategies will create and offer new services and with them, new jobs.

Economic Cycles

"An economist is an expert who will know tomorrow why the things he predicted yesterday didn't happen today."

- Laurence J. Peter, Canadian educator and hierarchiologist who formulated the Peter principle

With so many economists and predictions in the market, this statement very accurately describes how businesses can only make attempts at knowing the economy of the future. However, they can attempt to get as close to reality as possible and there are some companies that will get it right at some point in time.

Although there are economic models that try to predict what will happen, there are so many variables that make it impossible to predict at one hundred percent what the future will hold.

The principal indicator of whether an economic cycle is positive or negative is the gross domestic product (GDP). A positive GDP indicates a growth cycle, while a negative GDP in two or three consecutive trimesters indicates an economic recession. If the recession is prolonged, it's considered an economic crisis.

The GDP is defined as the value of all the services and all the final merchandise produced by companies and people who have worked within the territory of that economy for a determined period of time.

The objective of those in government in the economic policy arena is to achieve high growth rates, stability in prices and high levels of occupation.

The formula to value GDP is: **GDP = C + I + E + X – M**

Where **C** is the total value of national consumption; **I** is the gross formation of capital, also known as investment; **E** is public expenditure; **X** is the total value of exports; and **M** is the volume or value of imports.

Nominal GDP

Nominal GDP is the total monetary value of goods and services that a country produces in a determined period of time. This GDP is generally affected by the inflation of a dynamic economy, which means that part of the GDP or its growth is only due to inflation and that, in real terms, isn't what it appears to be at first.

Real GDP

Real GDP is the result of deflating the nominal GDP. It's what results from removing the effect of inflation from the nominal GDP. Under these conditions, it's possible to determine with precision the size of the real GDP and its effective growth relative to a reference period.

In a financial and economic crisis, GDP allows you to distinguish the economic cycle you are in. The sequence of each economic cycle is initiated with a crisis, which is followed by a depression stage, a recovery and reactivation stage, and a boom stage, which, inevitably, will be followed by a crisis.

It is important to highlight that economic crises are characterized by a combination of different factors:

- Production excess;
- The accentuation of contradictions and conflicts between different sectors of the economy;
- Growing difficulties on the part of economic agents to sell the goods and services they produce;
- Company bankruptcy;
- Lack of cash flow;
- Increases in unemployment and underemployment.

Why a Strategic Plan for Asset Management?

A lack of planning and an asset management policy brings about destabilization and unsustainability in many organizations. This is why many companies haven't made new investments or carried out efficient asset management (e.g., their plant stops and performing an overhaul and applying reliability from the design stage). Generally in this sense, plant stops don't finish on time or their costs are higher relative to what was budgeted.

Maintenance reliability is managed as a cost center and its associated processes are not sufficiently mature for implementation of true asset management and not just another fashion or a simple software implementation of enterprise asset management (EAM) or enterprise resource planning (ERP). This leaves the industry, with regard to its classification in asset management, as being in the past, which indicates that it registers high indices of corrective maintenance (CM) instead of preventive maintenance (PM), predictive maintenance (PdM) and proactive maintenance (PAM).

What strategies are there to find light at the end of the sustainability tunnel?

What would be required is an approach that strengthens the effectiveness and efficiencies of asset management, aligned to norms and standards like **ISO 55001, asset management systems**, and **BS EN16646, maintenance within physical asset management**, and without losing sight of the development of research, development and innovation. (R+D+I). Investing in R+D+I and implementation of new technologies strengthens integration and growth of personnel competencies and their connection with the different areas of the business. This creates short, medium and long-term strategies for good practices that allow you to build your dream.

In the case of asset management, the first step for an organization is to integrate maintenance, production and projects so these departments are NOT seen as centers of expenditure and zero profitability or as silos. In this sense, the goal is to preserve the functions of the asset in an efficient and efficacious way to generate value, which would then impact the final product and the global economy.

Innovation in the use of asset management practices can be seen as a source of additional business yield. A strategic plan initiated by an assessment is required, with tools like people, process, product (3Ps) or self-assessment methodology (SAM), to make a photograph of the current situation with regard to tangible, intangible, financial and non-financial assets, as well as the way in which things are done.

Maintenance is a significant part of direct costs of operations for companies. With profit margins becoming slimmer and slimmer, maintenance and operations are two of the few areas where a company can improve its profitability. Maintenance and operations have traditionally been managed as a cost to be minimized, rather than a **strategic process that could help the organization make decisions in terms of its asset management (e.g., replacement, investment, etc.) for the profitability of the business.**

The first step to take is to understand the complete economic reimbursement potential of an asset management program and its associated cost, assuming that:

- The optimization of a lifecycle of an asset depends on effective maintenance and operations.

- The management of maintenance and operations is a process and not merely technical matters.

An asset management program increases efficiency and the length of life for a company's equipment, therefore increasing profitability. These ideas form part of the management of the lifecycle of assets, as shown in Figure 3.

In order to fully understand the benefits of rerouting asset management, it is useful to define a model of management of the lifecycle's asset as a system of business management.

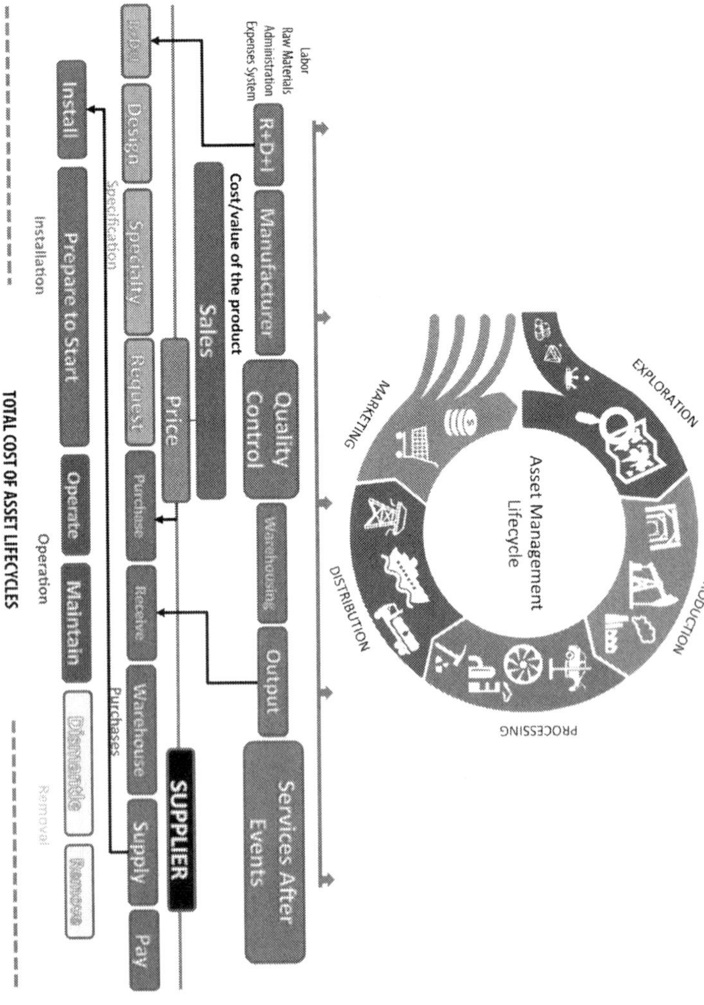

Figure 3: Management of asset lifecycle *(Amendola, L., 2004, 2015)*

Optimization of the Operations and Maintenance Phase

Optimal yield during this phase of the asset's lifecycle is only achieved in organizations that span a holistic focus, from lower to higher complexity. This brings about close and intimate work between the areas of operations and maintenance, given that these two areas are jointly enablers, allowing you to achieve the requirements of the business plan.

While there are many definitions of maintenance, it can be defined and directed as a process to obtain optimal reimbursements of expenses (capital). This is why you need to identify an asset management system as an integral part of the model of management of the asset's lifecycle, as defined previously.

During the operations and maintenance stages of an asset's lifecycle, the formula in Figure 4 can be used to obtain optimal performance. Optimal performance is equal to optimal availability multiplied by optimal efficiency.

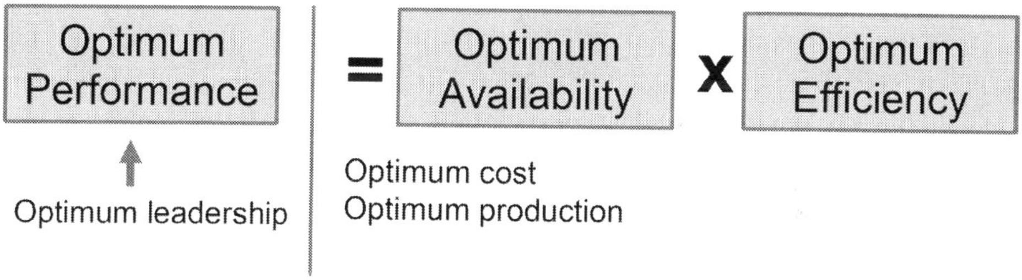

Figure 4: Optimal performance diagram

Additionally, in order to achieve optimal performance, these three critical factors are needed.

1. Preserving Asset Function

The assets of a plant should be directed and managed to achieve the goals that have been set by the directive, which must show itself to be more effective in minimizing costs. How can you achieve this? A strategy for asset management must be developed, centered on the asset's function. The function of the asset defines what is necessary to achieve the fulfillment of the operations' objectives. So, the efficacious management of assets is, basically, the preservation of asset function in order to fulfill the operations requirement, making reference to the preservation not only of the asset itself, as shown in Figure 5.

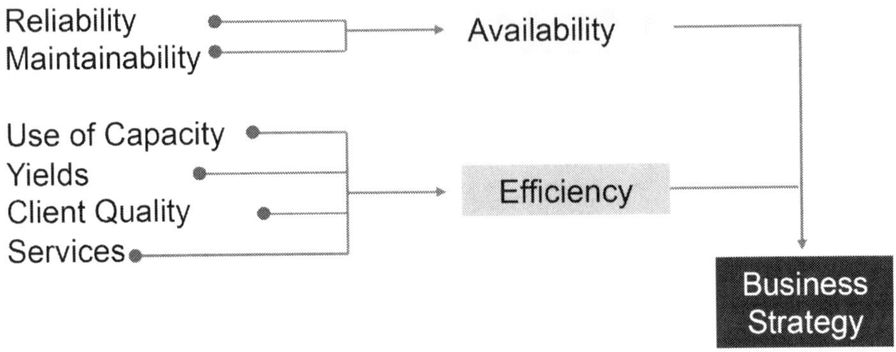

Figure 5: Business strategy scheme

The development of a strategy with this focus provides the method to define and manage a realistic and accurate maintenance and operations budget. This is basically a technical matter that has been made effective by the application of processes, such as the optimization of assets.

2. Maintaining Maintenance

Processes have to be established in an adequate way to efficiently manage maintenance activities, evaluate yield with regard to objectives, initiate some necessary improvement and perfect actions that involve processes and intellectual capital. The PMM Institute for Learning, an organization created by research specialists from both industry and academia that specializes in asset management and reliability and maintenance management, defines the process as the 3Ps (people, process, product), in which people, or the intellectual capital, is doubly important.

The process shows the connection of the entire business in a reasoned way, as a cycle of continual improvement. The perfecting actions to be put in place will be determined by the business needs that prevail in the stage of the asset's life.

This, too, is a technical matter, although it isn't commonly directed within an organization unless a model of management of the asset's lifecycle has been adopted. This is more easily achieved if the company uses a systems' focus for its own organization and if the management of QUALITY is developed within the organization.

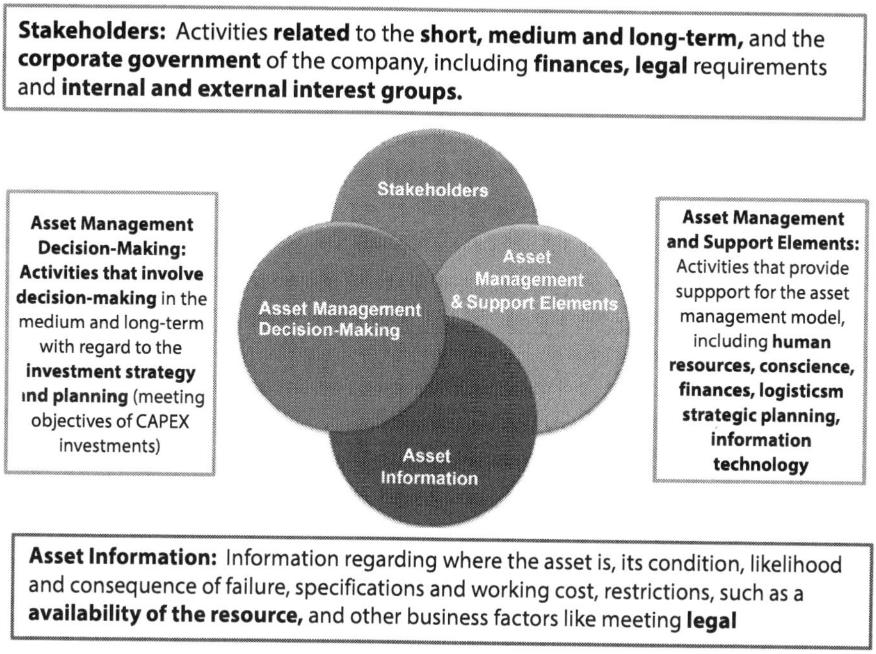

Figure 6: Asset management organization alignment model *(Amendola, 2015)*

3. Taking Strategy to Action "The Motor, People"

In order to achieve the maximum potential of actions executed in an efficacious way, employees should know and clearly understand their responsibilitics and objectives in terms of the asset management processes. With these criteria, people understand how and in what way to fulfill the objectives, which will bring about the achievement of global objectives and goals of the business. This is not simply a technical matter; it frequently happens that this proposal is not perceived as an integral part of asset management.

Personnel who are part of the directive and asset management are usually advised by the human resources doctrine within the organization. However, if this doctrine is poorly conducted and isn't aligned with the organization's needs (e.g., work processes, human talent and technology), it would limit proper performance of the asset, which would impact profitability of the company.

These factors are usually treated in an isolated way in some companies. Many organizations have spent millions of euros and dollars in EAM software, analysis of reliability programs and educating their work teams, but have yet to achieve the results the business requires. These poor results are motivated by a deficient connection between the three aforementioned critical factors, which do not allow for the management of the asset's lifecycle. Failures of this sort only strengthen people's perception that they have once more experienced one of those management directives, without concrete results. In this sense, one must not lose sight that maintenance and operations processes should provide the availability required by the business at optimal cost.

Advantages of Applying an Asset Management Strategy

When the work processes, human talent and technology factors converge, a synergistic management of assets in the business occurs and can be appreciated when these outcomes happen:

- The objectives of the company are used to make decisions regarding the use and care of assets.
- Operations and maintenance work together as teams to develop common goals.
- Performance and reliability objectives are directed toward the profitability of the company or business.
- All resources are optimized, not only maintenance resources.

Results obtained by organizations that have been successful in integrating the three factors as a part of their asset management system include these parameters:

- Benefit increases from twenty-five percent to sixty percent;
- Productivity increases from twenty percent to twenty-five percent;
- Equipment downtime (i.e., non-programmed stops) are minimized up to ninety-eight percent;
- Maintenance costs are reduced up to thirty percent.

Asset management needs to be considered as a system from the lowest to the highest complexity. This ensures good decisions are made coherently for the use and care of the equipment and are carried out to construct the best profitability for the business. The purpose of this system of management is to make sure assets are capable of achieving the performance required by the business, optimizing the lifecycle of the asset.

Chef's Recommendations:

There is enormous, unexplored potential in organizations to improve performance and profitability. Employing asset management practices in an efficacious manner guarantees the goals and objectives of the business are successfully met. This requires the whole company to manage assets throughout their entire lifecycle.

Enjoy every dish, don't eat everything in a hurry.

Taste the flavors well and you will be able to be critical as to what ingredient is missing or shouldn't be there.

THE DIFFERENCE BETWEEN ASSET MANAGEMENT AND MAINTENANCE RELIABILITY MANAGEMENT

Asset management is composed of six elements, as shown in Figure 7, along with the details of the sub-elements that compose operations and maintenance (O&M).

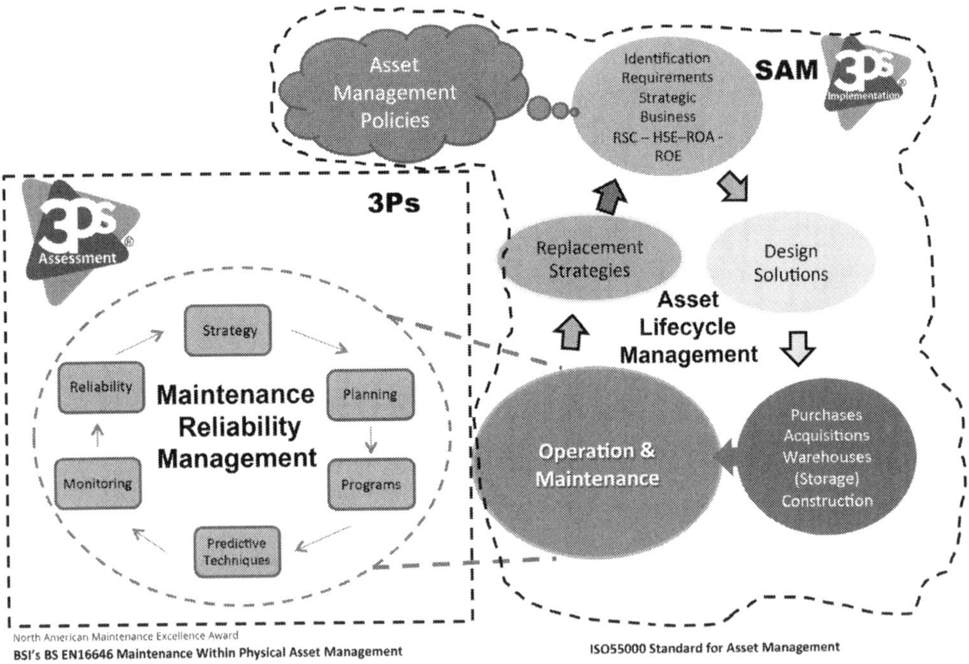

Figure 7: Asset lifecycle management model *(Amendola, L., 2012, 2015)*

The **first element** consists of identifying the strategic requirements of the business associated with corporate governance, corporate social responsibility (CSR), health, safety and environment (HSE), and goals and expectations of shareholders (i.e., return on assets (ROA) and return on capital employed (ROCE) indicators.

The **second element** is represented by the organization's plans and objectives, the management policy and the strategic plan for asset management, through which the structure for developing and implementing the objectives of the asset management strategies is defined. These, in turn, define the principles and mandatory requirements that are derived and consistent with the organization's strategic plan (ISO 55001: 2014).

The **third element** is the design of solutions related to the identification, evaluation and definition of the portfolio, programs and projects guided toward achieving the business goals or the development improvements in operations, the supply chain and optimization of the resources. In this third element, the cost evaluation of the asset's lifecycle and design reliability are crucial. Making sure of this from the initial stages helps the processes at the level of purchasing, acquisitions, warehousing, construction, operations and maintenance be fluid and optimal. This is what is called the union of capital expenditure (CAPEX) with operational expenditure (OPEX).

The **fourth element** is related to the process of purchases, acquisitions, warehouse management and construction.

The **fifth element** consists of the management of maintenance reliability. This element defines the strategy, planning, programming and development of predictive techniques, the monitoring of asset condition and performance, and the management of reliability that implies processes, operations and personnel.

The **sixth element** is related to the strategies for replacing assets that lead to the evaluation of updating assets on the basis of valuing costs of the cycle of life, risks and benefits, all aligned with the strategies and goals of the business.

In ISO 55000, maintenance management is related to managing the history of equipment failures in order to optimize the improvement and replacement of asset strategies, and define and manage future maintenance requirements. It also defines and differentiates asset management as the coordinated activity of an organization to generate value through its physical assets.

In this same sense, in a more general and strategic way, asset management is designed to connect higher directives with the tactical part using a concept called line of sight.

The reference framework of AM requires valuing and defining risk so it is acceptable and understood by all levels of the organization. This provides the alignment of decision-making at all levels of the organization to generate value through the assets at an acceptable level of risk.

ISO 55000 Standard for Asset Management and BS EN16646 Maintenance Within Physical Asset Management

The ISO 55000 is the specific standard for asset management. This norm makes a relationship between key terms: asset portfolio, asset management system, asset management and organization management. The standard is composed of ten key elements and twenty-three requirements to cover the breadth of asset management of an organization. These key elements and requirements provide the context and global direction of activities of an organization that include the activities of asset management.

The EN 16646 is a European norm that introduces the relationship between the system of strategic plan management and maintenance in an organization and describes the interrelationships between the process of maintenance and other processes of asset management. It is directed at defining the role and importance of maintenance within the system of physical asset management, covering the whole lifecycle of the asset. This European norm has applicability in production organizations of all sizes. The objective of the norm is to guide and recommend; it is not destined to be used for certification or contractual use.

In this same sense, the process of maintenance provides contributions to the process of asset management:

a. Reliability characteristics of the asset or asset system;
b. Reliability, maintainability and safety will be known by the directives in order to make decisions related with the strategic plan of the organization;
c. Characteristics of asset lifecycle costs, including maintenance costs, direct and indirect costs, and relevant information for asset management;
d. Impact of asset management strategies, including the relationship between corrective and preventive actions, and compensation between actions at short and long terms of the assets;

e. Impact of maintenance strategies and activities on asset management policy, strategies and plans; an example of this is the definition of the level of required competencies, according to maintenance actions, that will help make decisions on subcontracting and the level of maintenance.

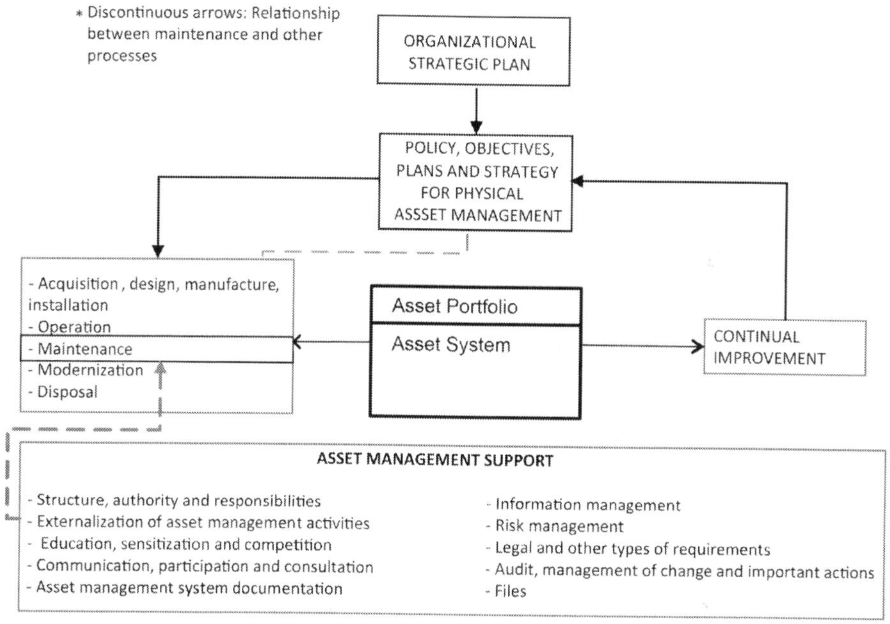

Figure 8: Interrelations between maintenance processes and other processes of the asset management system, EN16646 Maintenance Within Physical Asset Management

Asset Management as an Impulse to Business

High, continuous profitability of assets in industrial facilities is essential to meet production demands, comply with safety and environmental regulations and initiatives, limit production losses and successfully accomplish the optimization of operational costs.

The goal is to take reactive maintenance strategies to proactive ones that maximize the uptime and minimize failures of the equipment. To obtain that end, many organizations dedicate a large quantity of time and money to deploy the best technologies and experts in the field only to find themselves stuck in reactive mode. For example, an executive for one of the most important petrochemical companies in the world pointed out that:

"We went out in search for and bought the best solutions for asset management. Afterward, we hired experts to use the productive solutions. Even so, years later we continue to be sixty percent reactive."

How Can Such a Situation Be Avoided?

The most recent evidence suggests that it is possible to move toward a state that is highly proactive by implementing a very structured focus, integrated and broad in relation to asset management, where all parts of an organization are integrated through the management of assets' lifecycles.

Those who have worked in the industry for many years will remember when safety programs and initiatives were introduced at a large scale and the focus of a sole understanding of safety, accidents and incidents was a common thing. Now, they are considered unacceptable. Safety is a strategic goal for management, both in execution and evaluation by way of metrics, where improvement is required and new strategies for asset management are created and implemented. Safety is considered in system design and prevails in daily operations, execution of work tasks and routine department meetings.

Possibly most important of all, safety has become a goal for companies in which workers at each and every level provide data on their performance. Upon entering through the main entrance of a company, you will probably see a sign that states when the last injury was in detailed hours, days, or maybe years. The main point is in places where optimum safety yield has been obtained, you will find structured programs that are adequately integrated, but are also very broad.

Asset management is very similar to the joint drivers of business that were the origin of the first safety initiatives. First, significant financial incentives exist to maintain high asset yield. In the majority of facilities, the loss of money through non-production prevails, a situation created by the non-programmed interruption of service due to insufficient or inadequate asset yield. According to an industry survey, a high-level refinery reported an average of ten failures a day, or approximately thirty-six hundred annual failures, related to work orders. The average cost of each failure is reported at $3,963. This translates into more than $14 million annually.

In the same survey, it was reported that production losses generally duplicated the cost of failures related to work orders. As such, the loss production opportunity (LPO) costs for this refinery facility was more than $28 million. Therefore, safety and environmental issues are major preoccupations of production facilities. So...why aren't assets failures?

Chef's Recommendations:

Recognize industry drivers...

There are typical and specific drivers in industry that take an organization toward a vision of asset management that are not only maintenance reliability. And that's where the difference lies. These include:

- Reductions in LPOs, which are generally unexpected events that happen as a result of an incapacity to meet production demands;
- Safety initiatives that demand safe and reliable operations of the process;
- Environmental and health initiatives that demand, for example, a reduction in volatile organic compound (VOC) leaks;
- Net return and meeting of key goals of ROA, ROCE and return of capital (ROC);
- Economic reduction dollars for maintenance and unexpected stops or interruptions, planned or programmed work;
- Meeting of production demands and client satisfaction with one hundred percent on time delivery;
- Own objectives of reliability, availability and maintenance capacity.

When you manage to have asset management occupy a place like safety does (i.e., where accidents and incidents are unacceptable), you will really be implementing real asset management.

What would happen if non-generation of value is defined as unacceptable?

Creative Leadership

The Ability to Change the Company's Status Quo

The majority of businesspeople want their businesses to triumph and sweep competitors. They search for that blue ocean in which competition between companies is left to the side, broadening the market through innovation, creativity and resilience. On the other hand is the red ocean, representing companies that must have their limits clearly marked and their competition defined. Their objective is to best their rival and win a position in the market. They are constantly exposed to the arrival of new competitors that decrease their growth possibilities. Generally, a red ocean is the reality of every business. The characteristics of red ocean industries are competition in existing market spaces and the competition challenge, aligning their strategy at low cost while exploiting at maximum capacity market demand.

The task is to carry through an idea of implementing asset management that is successfully put into practice. Most times, success doesn't hide a strike of luck or a genius idea. What is behind it is a lot of analysis, teamwork and collaboration.

"The test of innovation lies not in its novelty, its scientific content, or its cleverness. It lies in its success in the marketplace."

-Peter Drucker, management consultant, educator and author

When a business doesn't work, you generally don't stop to think about what it is that you do, who you go to and what you want to achieve. You think innovation is the great savior and consists of finding something new that will attract the client, but you fail because you aren't conscious of what you have and don't plan for the variations you need. You need to ask yourself, how can you invent, design and apply an efficient model for asset management in a systematic way? How should you challenge and transform obsolete models? And, how can you convert visionary ideas?

To answer these formulated questions, important ingredients are missing: promoting and managing creativity, and more concretely, developing creative leadership for asset management.

Experience has shown that in the company environment, it is very important to learn to work outside your comfort zone.

The Frog and the Comfort Zone

The natural habitat of a frog is water. So, if you put a frog in a container with cold water, it's likely to stay there and enjoy its new environment. Basically, that's the environment in which it finds pleasure and comfort. But, if you put a frog in a container with hot water, it will instantly respond by jumping out of it because that isn't its natural habitat. Now, here's a valuable aspect that may interest you: If you place the container of cold water on a heater and slowly heat it, the frog will continue to feel comfortable and find the experience pleasant because it feels warm and will stay there. When you increase the heat even further, it still feels safe and warm until it is cooked and dies.

This example shows that comfort isn't always a zone, but when change comes, that place will slowly become a danger zone if you continue in it.

Most people and organizations are in their comfort zone because that is their natural habitat and they feel safe remaining there. But it's a mentality of: "I'm winning, but I'm losing opportunities to win." Just like the frog that finally died in boiling water, organizations refuse to jump outside their pleasure area and prefer to stay in their comfort zone because it's warmer and more comfortable every time.

One must take into account that nature is always in a constant state of movement and change, so if you prefer to stay in a comfort zone and not respond to change, then you most likely will become stuck in routines and not progress. According to the law of nature, when you go against the current of life and don't respond to change, in a short period, you will find the danger zone and frankly, have a bad time. Developing lateral thinking to find solutions to problems, having an open mind, forgetting conventional wisdom and knowing how to create a work environment that inspires your team and drives it to collaborate, that's creative leadership.

Based on research in articles, journals and schools, creative leadership originated in Holland in a business school specifically for the development of this area, called THNK, The Amsterdam School of Creative Leadership.

The appearance of creative leadership centers in companies and the higher prominence that companies are giving to these matters in corporate education show the increasing importance that creative leadership has in asset management in times of changes in the economic cycle.

More and more organizations are demanding that the profile of the asset manager be someone with a lot of curiosity, passion and a will to motivate teams. The average lifespan of a company decades ago was fifty years. Now, with luck, it will get to be ten years. One of the reasons is the lack of creative leaders; companies have increasing difficulties in finding them.

Characteristics of the New Asset Manager Director / Manager

There are many definitions of creativity and even debate over the similarities and differences between creativity and innovation. However, there is consensus over what is and what stops creative leadership. According to THNK, it is composed of five key aspects:

1. **Exploratory mentality** – Curiosity, capacity to find inspiration in different sources and the ability to transform uncertainty into a company asset.
2. **Passion and objectives** – A creative leader knows what he/she wants to find and why. This person knows himself/herself, the virtues and defects, and leads in a natural way.

3. **Team direction** – Knows how to build multidisciplinary teams and gives these teams power to innovate. More than a boss, he/she is a guide.
4. **Orientation towards results** – Creativity is useless without results. In order to achieve them, a creative leader is capable of convincing the organization of the importance of change and to turn an idea into a business.
5. **Vision** – Not afraid of being a pioneer, to risk, to propose disruptive solutions and fight to find a better future.

What Should the Present and Future Leadership Ability Be?

According to an IBM study carried out on fifteen hundred delegate counselors in numerous countries, sixty percent identified creativity as the leadership ability that would be most important in the future, above that of integrity and global thinking. The capacity to change the company's status quo with strategies never before put in practice, feeling comfortable with uncertainty and turning it into an advantage, or knowing how to innovate in processes, products and services are some of the characteristics of a creative leader.

Yet, the problem lies in rigid company structures that, instead of stimulating creativity, tend to scare it away. The majority of organizations force ideas to fit into a business plan.

Disruptive ideas are those that produce a sudden break, like thinking the unthinkable or surprising the market with products that are not very conventional. Many organizations dedicate a lot of money and resources to get ahead of the competition with gradual changes in their products and services. This is a characteristic mostly of mature sectors that choose gradual change because it's the one that favors their current business model. Few are inclined to invest money to modify current operations and create new products that compete with products they have always had. These companies become complacent and stop innovating, resulting in their clients abandoning them for a new product that no one saw coming.

Becoming different through gradual change and not by disruptive innovation means becoming different to stay on the outside. Simply put, companies cannot allow themselves to wait for the competition to drive them into a corner. They always must be ready to propose bold bets in the implementation of asset management. Instead of differentiate or die, what must be done is differentiate as much as you want, as long as you find a way to be unique in what you do. In other words, fit nowhere. Companies should make their functioning flexible in order to allow creativity to flow.

The spirit of belonging and obsessive consensus within the team can become a company pathology. But, in order for it not to drown imagination and hope or truncate new opportunities, **employees must be challenged to raise their voices and question ideas.**

Teamwork is fashionable. Companies' management manuals proclaim the bonanza of belonging and a shared effort. And it's true, you give your best when you are committed to an idea, a project, or a team. However, there is a thin red line that, if crossed, can turn the feeling of belonging into an organizational disease that causes important company errors.

It's what U.S. psychologist Irving Janis called group thinking in 1972: a way of thinking that people adopt when profoundly involved in a group. This desire to belong drives group members to try to minimize conflict and achieve consensus without critically testing, analyzing, or evaluating consensus ideas. Evidently, the group thinking term is still applicable in today's times.

Team or Herd?

Organizations have the duty and responsibility to create different spaces that allow their professionals to connect and create in a different way. But, one mustn't confuse a good work atmosphere with becoming a herd where there are no dissonant voices. The dangers of group thinking affect large and small companies. The latter tend to be led by authoritarian directors and managers who don't tolerate discrepancy, while in the former, this type of behavior is extended through excess confidence in the directive that, backed by their successes, believe themselves to be invaluable.

In this context, you could say that meetings too often turn into mere theater, where, before beginning, a pact is formed about the line of acting that is desired. Additionally, listening to all voices and questioning proposals slow down decision-making, whereas in the work market, speed takes all. Companies no longer compete among themselves, they compete against speed.

To avoid this lack of critical thinking that ends up disillusioning and demotivating employees, you must incite the group to search for new challenges. This means training your imagination, strengthening the synergies of creativity collaboration and celebrating innovations and the impacts they have.

It is easy to put a series of remedies in practice. First, create a devil's advocate figure, a role that rotates in each meeting and criticizes what is said and not who says it. Next, research your competitors as much as possible because forgetting them doesn't result in good things. Then, count on the collaboration of experts, inside and outside the company, to provide another point of view. Lastly, do not decide everything in a small group.

Black Sheep: Where Are They? I Want One!

Employees, therefore, play a fundamental role. They are the ones who must accept the challenge of raising their hand and be bold enough to disagree and question things. Obviously, this way of acting assumes becoming the black sheep of the herd, the uncordial professional who says, "Yes, but..." There resides the problem, because not many employees are willing to come out of their comfort zone and put themselves in eye view of the boss and coworkers and accept most of the reprimands.

However, in good and bad economies, the time has come to raise voices. Many companies are warming up to destroying **group thinking** because they have noticed that complacency and consensus without previous discussion fail to provide the solutions they need. That's why, now more than ever, you need dissidents or rebels willing to question norms because in their hands rest the possibility of bringing about a new environment.

Putting these ideas into practice begins with the definition of the business model. Think about what your company's differentiating characteristics are. Review everything that is done in a simple way that everyone can understand. Create a common language that eases descriptions and debate. Without a common base and without talking about the same thing, you can't begin to develop new alternatives. Expressing what it is you want to do to all involved is one of the most powerful tools.

Another fundamental aspect to give a new focus to the company is observing existing business models. Studying and analyzing them in detail can help you find the keys and patterns to create your own.

Innovation Does Not Belong to R&D Departments!

The design process is one of the crucial moments in the search for innovation. So, you should be capable of imagining that which doesn't exist. Often, there is a tendency to think that it is the realm of specialists, that is, the research and development (R&D) departments, but that isn't so. All professionals can and should provide ideas to design new ways to work or a new product to produce. Obviously, the most difficult thing is to innovate in consolidated companies. One of the challenges is to ignore status quo and dissipate doubts over operative matters in order to generate truly new ideas.

Chef's Recommendations:

Another workhorse is the creation of a good team. On occasion, directors are too elitist; a work group must be diverse, have professionals of all levels, and departments and people outside the company. Among the multiple aspects, communication should not be missing. Describing all that is required to everyone is one of the most powerful tools of the business world.

But without a doubt, one of the most decisive moments is putting things in practice, the execution. In this phase, coordinating the coexistence of new and old models is fundamental. This is a stage that is usually not contemplated, however, it is crucial for achieving success. The keys are achieving a creative leadership focus and having the capacity to change the company's status quo.

Innovation has nothing to do with how many dollars have been invested in R&D. For instance, when Apple® premiered the Mac® computer, IBM® spent at least one hundred times more in R&D. To paraphrase Steve Jobs, co-founder, chairman and CEO of Apple Inc., it's not a matter of quantity, but of the people you have, how you guide them and how much you gain.

PREPARATION FOR ASSET MANAGEMENT

Provolone and Pancetta Brochettes

Preparation

1. Cut the provolone in 24 small cubes
2. Cut each slice of smoked pancetta in half, lengthwise, and wrap it around each cube, crossed to cover all the provolone.
3. Place on each skewer half an olive, 1 prepared cube and half a cherry tomato.
4. Put in the refrigerator for 2 to 3 hours.
5. Before serving, place them on an oven tray, spray with olive oil and bake for a few minutes on high temperature.

Ingredients

- 14 ounces provolone cheese, cut thickly
- 24 slices of smoked pancetta
- 12 cherry tomatoes, cut in half
- 12 green olives, cut in half
- 24 brochette skewers
- Olive oil

Chef's Comments:

A small mouthful prepares the stomach for all that is to come next. It is the anteroom for a mound of sensory reactions that transport you to your deepest memories. It is a great pleasure to eat food made with quality products in small quantities. It's worthwhile to be left wanting.

Kitchen and Asset Management Reflection:

Take a cue from the chef's kitchen. Focus on quality and small accomplishments and leave them wanting more. That is how you should begin the process for implementing asset management.

Just as a chef explains to those who will eat what plates they will be tasting, you should explain to your collaborators the process of asset management and their participation in it.

Main Dish

ASSET MANAGEMENT MODEL AND MATURITY

Maturity in Organizations

Most dictionaries define maturity as the development level of a person, organization, etc. Merriam-Webster defines maturity as the "quality or state of being mature, perfect, completely developed, or focused on perfection."

The Project Management Institute (PMI®) defines maturity as "the degree to which an organization practices project management."

Many other experts in the field have created their own definitions of maturity. Here is a sampling of them:

- Achieving maturity means reaching the point in which expected evolution is achieved.
- Maturity involves a product or service in perfect condition.
- Maturity is the development of systems and processes that are repetitive in nature and provide a high probability that each project will be a success. (However, repetitive processes and systems are not, by themselves, a guarantee of success. They merely increase its possibility.)
- Maturity is the state in which the organization is in a condition to achieve its objectives.

According to the guide offered by Organizational Project Management Maturity Model (OPM3®), a company can apply organization to itself as a whole or to one specific unit of the business, functional groups, departments, or subgroups. Project management of a company consists of systematic management of its projects, programs and portfolios to achieve its strategic goals.

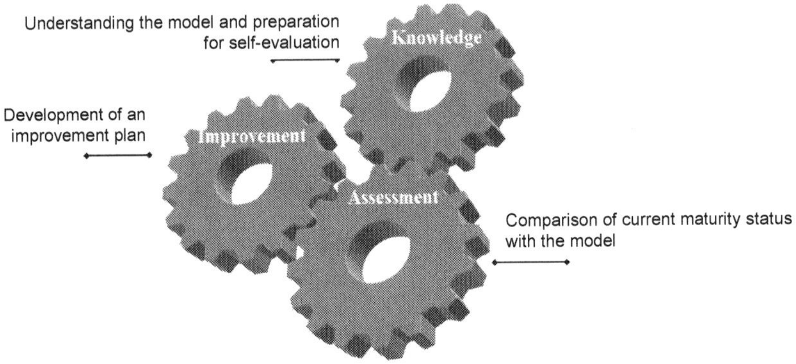

Figure 9: Organizational project management maturity model (OPM3)

According to many studies and research projects, there is a positive relationship between maturity and success in an organization.

The Greek philosopher Aristotle said: ***"We are what we repeatedly do. Excellence, then, is not an act but a habit."***

In 1997, PMI® charged lecturers William Ibbs and Justin Reginato of the University of California at Berkeley with the evaluation of fifty-two organizations in the United States. The results were published in 1998 with these conclusions:

- The more mature companies in project management have better yields in their projects.
- Maturity in project management is strongly related with the planning terms, costs and most predictable results.
- Companies with good project management have fewer direct costs than companies with poorer project management.

What Is a Model?

According to the Royal Spanish Academy of Language, a model is defined as:

- Archetype or point of reference to be imitated or reproduced;
- Small representation of something;
- Theoretical scheme, generally of the mathematical form, of a system or a complex reality, like the economic evolution of a country that is elaborated to facilitate its understanding and the study of its behavior.

On the other hand, author Sinan Si Alhir defines a model as an abstraction of a system or context.

A model defines steps or stages, implies changes and progression. Continual improvement must be guided toward the development of capacities following these steps or stages. The level of maturity is generally determined through an official maturity model. Once the level of maturity has been established, it can be used as a road map to improve specific processes in the organization.

Maturity models have their origin in the field of total quality management (TQM). In order to drive improvement in an organization, they need profound knowledge of the current situation and what the organization aspires to achieve.

A maturity model provides a systematic framework to carry out comparative evaluation and improvement of yield. Through different, progressive levels of maturity, a maturity model helps define, understand and measure an organization's processes and efficiencies. Additionally, maturity models are an essential tool to evaluate real capacities of an organization and help implement changes and improvements in a structured way.

Maturity models also improve the organization's positioning and help it find better solutions for change. Project management supports the business strategy, while maturity worries about continual improvement of processes.

According to Harold Kerzner, senior executive director for project management at the International Institute for Learning (IIL), there are driving forces that lead management in the correct direction and route the organization toward maturity in project management. The driving forces come out of real problems and business opportunities that require routing through solid practices.

According to author Gutenberg de Araujo Silveira, there are six frequent driving forces:

- **Strategic projects:** Organizations are directed toward project management in view of investments. Poorly budgeted projects can impact results and promote financial and economic disequilibrium in organizations. In the face of this, organizations need to effectively plan their investments, with project management the best medium for this.
- **Client expectations:** Companies don't buy products or services, but rather complete solutions that are well administered, managed and have quality. Clients expect better management on the part of their providers. That means providers need to administer the contracts effectively and efficiently using project management.
- **Competitiveness:** This depends on two situations: (1) Internal – the costs are properly dimensioned, associated with performance; (2) External – the prices and quality can interfere in competitiveness and, therefore, in market share. Executives want their employees to prioritize external competition over internal.
- **Understanding and commitment of executive managers:** This driving force depends on executive ability to overcome internal barriers and implement good practices in project management, obtaining acceptance and commitment from participants of an organization from top to bottom.
- **Development of new products:** Due to more structured processes and better practices in project management, companies can create and commercialize their products and services, optimizing their investment.
- **Efficiency and effectiveness:** These are associated with the speed in which changes of practices and customs are implemented in organizations, with the objective of achieving higher competitiveness.

These driving forces are directed toward survival and success of the organization, as long as they are responded to quickly due to the turbulent and discontinuous environment in which companies live. When organizations recognize survival as an objective, project management becomes easier.

The level of maturity varies in each organization according to management type, company structure and the relationship among its members. The culture of the organization and the nature of the business define how much time is necessary to achieve maturity in project management. All companies go through their own process of maturity and need constant perfecting in order to maintain that level.

The three pillars to the maturity of an organization are competence, commitment and coordination, which are key factors for the success of projects. Maturity, therefore, is not a state, but an objective that assures more capacities, economic gains and client satisfaction.

Maturity models are also defined as abstract, with these benefits:

- Allows organizations to benchmark with other organizations, internal or external.
- Allows people outside the organization to be certain of its potential.
- Offers an improvement path for organizations.

What Does Increasing the Maturity Level Provide?

- A reduction in a variety of processes and an improvement in project and organizational yield;
- Higher productivity and client satisfaction;
- Better quality and a reduction in costs of quality.
- Improvement in employee morale;
- Reduction in defects and costs;
- A substantial return on investment.

Each model has a different emphasis on how it achieves maturity in each of the different levels of the organization. Each organization must choose the model to follow according to its own needs or create its own model.

Determining the correct maturity level is no easy task, given that it involves diverse factors, such as individual interviews, process evaluations, standards, knowledge and company culture. Therefore, it's important to use an evaluation tool that has been tried and demonstrated with regard to consistency in the type of results it provides. Maturity models mustn't be seen as models that solve problems, but rather a path to advancement in which project management abilities can be improved.

Progress in maturity levels are evolutionary steps with a specific focus and measurable goals that allow benefits to be obtained within a predetermined period of time, generally a few months. On another hand, companies mustn't fight to obtain the highest maturity level, but rather to achieve a minimum level in which the desired benefits and results are achieved.

In the real world, a fully mature organization doesn't exist. It can be argued that no organization has ever achieved absolute maturity and none ever will. However, it's useful to describe maturity of organizations in a way that can be measured or characterized. As a result, maturity models have been designed to evaluate the level of maturity of organizations.

Types of Maturity Levels

Many look toward Philip B. Crosby for the fundamentals of organizational maturity. He conceived the Quality Management Maturity Grid (QMMG), which is based on five incremental levels of maturity for the adoption of quality concepts in an organization.

Another is a general structure called portfolio, program and project management maturity model (P3M3®), which contains three different models: portfolio management maturity model (PfM3), program management maturity model (PgM3) and project management maturity model (PjM3). Although connected, there are no interdependencies among these models, which allows independent evaluation of any of the specific disciplines.

For example, the ability to manage the organization's programs can be more developed than the abilities for project management because the model for project management can be used as an independent tool in the search to improve in this area.

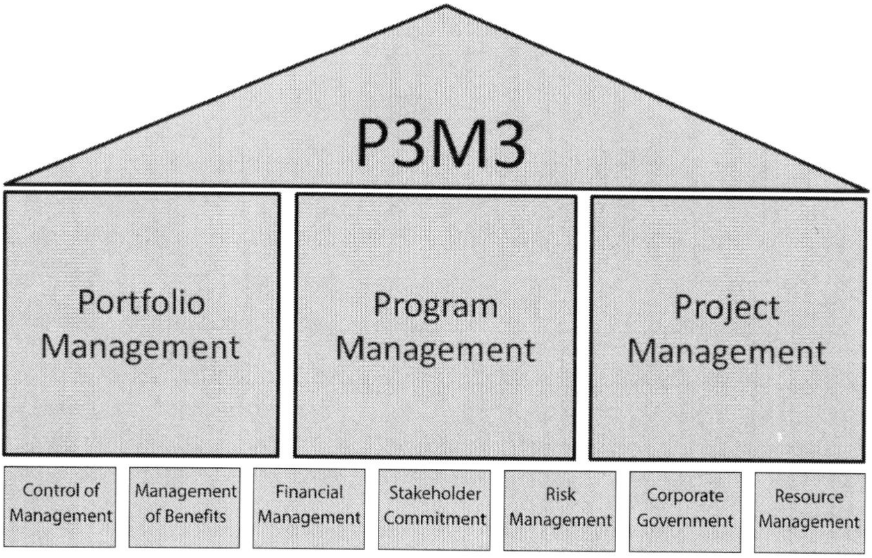

Figure 10: Portfolio, program and project management maturity model (P3M3®)

Each model uses a maturity scheme that has five levels. They are:

Level 1 – Awareness of the process;
Level 2 – Repeatable process;
Level 3 – Defined process;
Level 4 – Managed process;
Level 5 – Optimized process.

P3M3® is centered on seven process perspectives that exist within the three models and can be evaluated through the five maturity levels. The flexibility of P3M3® allows organizations to review all the process perspectives in the three models of portfolio, program and project management, but also review only one or several of the process perspectives, be it through the three models or in only one or two of them.

The P3M3® self-evaluation can be used in many ways, for example:

- Providing a basic introduction to the general vision of the P3M3® reach;

- Measuring the current level of an organization's maturity with respect to the portfolio, program and/or project management;
- Obtaining an understanding of the key practices in the portfolio, program and project management process;
- Identifying the key practices that need to be introduced within an organization to improve the capacity of processes and achieve the next maturity level;
- Understanding and improving an organization's capacity to manage its portfolio, programs and projects more effectively;
- Completing the nine questions in the self-evaluation questionnaire to obtain a relatively quick evaluation of the organization's current maturity with respect to portfolio, programs and/or project management;
- Making a decision based on the evaluation as to whether its reach is limited to a determined combination of portfolio and/or program and/or project management. For example, an organization can evaluate only the management of projects, programs and project management. A second decision could be about reach in determining the limits of the organization that will be reviewed, for example, the entire organization, a particular division, or just one department.

Management Models

Two types of management models exist:

- Concentric Model – Actions are joint, systematic and by layers. Its end is interactive.
- Linear Model – Actions are ordered by precedence and are systematic. Its end is less interactive.

Characteristics of concentric models:

- The actions act at once in a very systematic way.
- Can act in groups of actions that have consequences on others that are closer to the end.

- The end is very interactive with the previous level and coordination is key. Figure 11 shows this type of model.
- Functions act by levels. One over the others. All seem important, the center is vision and strategy.
- Management depends on good relationships with clients.
- Management identifies with seven "forces" (client, environment, system, etc.) that interact at once. There is no argument line.
- Mixes competencies with activities with organization, objectives, etc. (leadership, management of terms, project cycle, education, etc.). It's a system with elements of different characteristics.

Figure 11: Concentric model *(Cleland, David I., 1999)*

Characteristics of the convergent, linear model "closed":

- Actions are produced one after the other, although a systematic character is preserved. In the end, you get access via more than one avenue and it may not represent the conclusion, but the procedure for it.

- It's based on four pillars: division of labor, functions, structure and control. It doesn't mention the client.

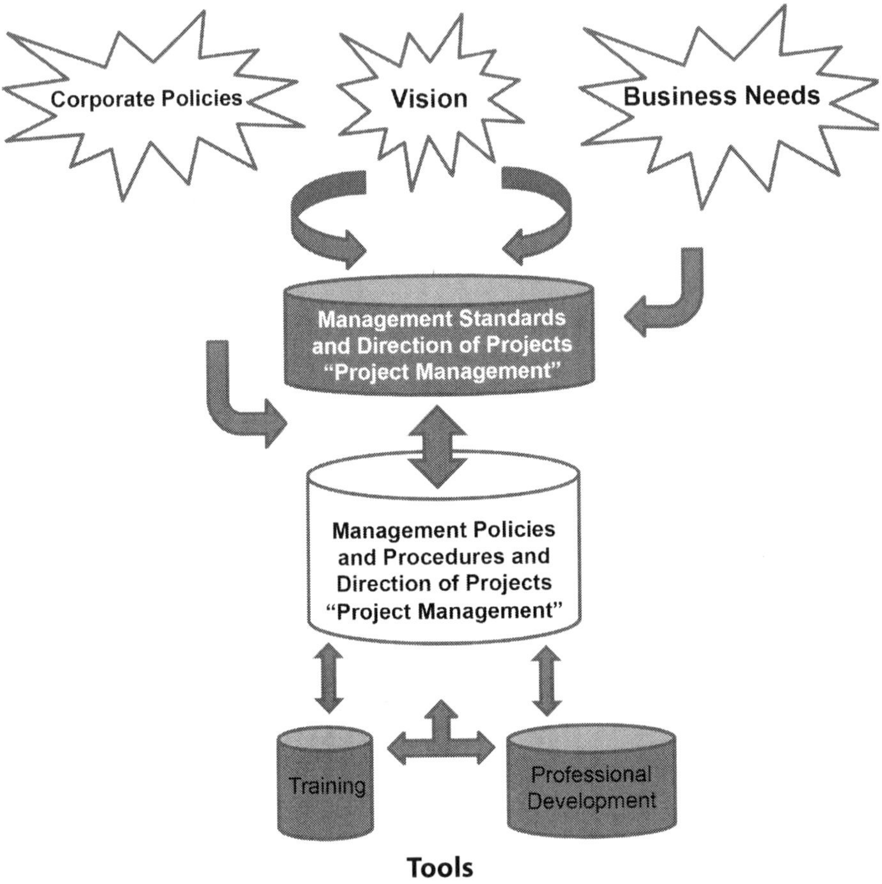

Figure 12: Convergent linear model *(Duell, Garry, 2000)*

Characteristics of the divergent, linear model "open":

- Processes model. Ends with the delivery to the client. Satisfaction is measured at the end of the process.
- What is important is the project plan, the satisfaction of the client and the integration of actions.

It's important for the physical asset management model to be seen as a key process and a part that determines the value chain of a company.

A structured focus in the models and methodologies allows for the management of assets from an organized viewpoint, centered on the creation of value. In this new way of seeing asset management, it's important to observe closely and comment on several processes that, jointly, make the activity of asset management a strategic process that influences businesses' profitability. Seen another way, this focus will allow you to structure an asset system that is aligned with the context of the organization and the interested parties (i.e., stakeholders), with the plans and objectives of the organization, asset management policies, the strategic plan and objectives of asset management and its connection with the plans of the asset management (i.e., asset portfolio) without losing sight of the evaluation of performance and improvements in order to align operative, tactic and strategic company plans.

Practically all companies, in all parts of the world, are setting their sights on how to design and implement an asset management model, as is the case of capital intensive companies. CEOs and general managers want to search for alternatives and strategies that support the optimization and efficiency of their assets and processes, all with the goal of remaining competitive in a global economy.

I propose the development of models and methodologies of integral asset management that constitute a unique combination of knowledge, services and tools to benefit organizations in the industrial sector. The intent of these models and methodologies to be designed, implemented and sustained is for joint work to be carried out between external experts and the company in order to offer at the global level a complete set of strategic and tactical services for the integral management of physical assets.

The strategic objectives for the design of a model for integral physical asset management are:

1. **Repeatable:** It can be explained to personnel involved and easily imitated or followed, always assuring it is current and adapted to the needs of the business.
2. **Establish the vision and mission:** Goals and objectives aligned with the organization's asset management model must be established.
3. **Know the current state and the future of assets:** Knowing where

you are starting from (e.g., organization, resources, capacities, processes, etc.) in order to use this state as a base reference for analysis of the lifecycle.

4. **Establish quantifiable objectives:** Start from the vision, establish milestones and require documents to be handed in to allow follow-up of the process.
5. **Planning:** Establish a plan for continual improvement (i.e., evaluation of yield) that determines the actions necessary to obtain the desired objectives of asset management at the predetermined quality.
6. **Verifying:** Determine if the strategic asset management plans have been carried through to their connection with the strategic plans of the company and if the processes established in asset management planning and implementation have been followed.
7. **Integrate management of change (MOC):** Assure that the changes made become part of the organization's culture, allowing you to reinitiate the cycle with a new energy.

Model for the Management of Physical Assets

In order to align physical asset management business strategies in industry, you first must create a statement that describes a purpose, a mission, a reason for being; it should become a management philosophy and the base for constructing a model. Without a statement of this type, you risk becoming an area of services oriented toward merely covering your clients' expectations and not generating extra value, defining and positioning the organization, or making the organization efficient. So, you must give form and focus to management, or in other words, orient asset services toward the client.

The integral physical asset management's reason for being is none other than the coordination of activities of an organization to create value through its physical assets. The generation of value makes references to the balance between costs, risks, opportunities and benefits of performance (ISO 55000:2014). This means you must avoid unpredicted asset failures and, at the same time, have your operations and maintenance services to clients carried out in optimal timeframes and at reasonable costs.

Once the objectives of an asset management model have been defined, you must begin to define the inputs required for the model.

Many of you have heard of the model called input, process and product. After all, it is not possible to refer to the activity of integral asset management without it.

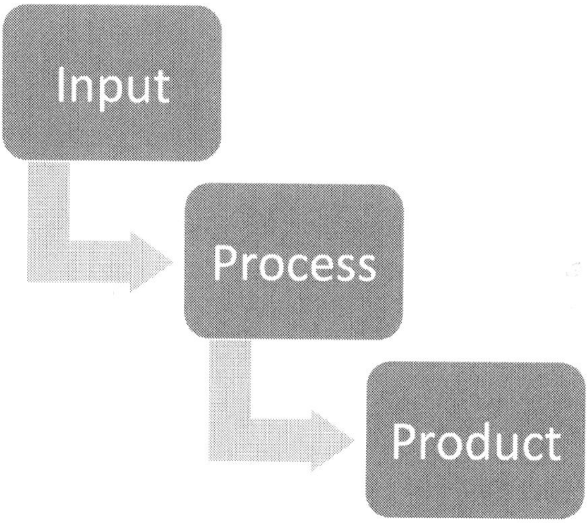

Figure 13: Asset management activity flow *(Amendola, 2011)*

Input includes the context of the organization and the interested parties (i.e., stakeholders), plans and objectives of the organization, asset management policies and the strategic plan for asset management.

Process includes the plans for asset management (i.e., asset portfolios).

Product is the implementation of the asset management plans, the evaluation of performance and the improvements to align the company's operational, tactic and strategic plans, as shown in Figure 14.

Figure 14: Integration Process *(Amendola, 2011)*

What should be included in asset management? The management itself can depend on the type of business, the company strategy, the level of results, the environment where the business develops, etc. In any case, it should always try to maximize operational reliability of the assets, understanding maximization as the optimization of cost-benefit-risk or, better said, optimizing expenditure in operations and maintenance up to where it is possible, without sacrificing the integrity of people and the environment.

Now that you have a basic structure, you are ready to propose the development of the model. This book presents, in a general way, the processes required by the model. It's important to mention that what is presented is only a guide based on industrial, academic and research experience accumulated by me and my team.

Steps for Designing an Asset Management Model

1. **Define and agree on needs:** The first step toward a successful design of an asset management model is to recognize within the core of the organization that there is a need to define a management model to orient and guide the company's activities.
2. **Define functions:** The objective is to identify the functions of integral asset management and the strategic objectives necessary to align with business objectives. In this phase, the vision and mission of asset management are reviewed. A common error committed in this stage of the process is not involving all levels of the organization. Consequently, the vision, mission and strategic objectives of the new management model are not shared by all levels and its implementation becomes traumatic, slow and costly.
3. **Define processes, people and technology:** Once the functions are defined, you must review the business areas associated with processes, people and technology in order to support the functions and strategic objectives that have been established.
4. **Define the evolution of the processes:** Once the strategic objectives are defined, the macro processes and business areas that will be part of integral asset management must be defined in a process map. This map must be followed by the organization in order to achieve evolution and continual improvement of each of the

business areas. This means that programs, projects, action plans and tasks must be defined in a way that allow continual evolution of the organization within the defined framework of evolution (i.e., the integral asset management model).

5. **Support tools:** At this point, an asset management model exists that will serve as a guide for the management of assets. However, the philosophical model and the definition of processes of improvement are not, in themselves, sufficient enough to achieve effective transformation of the management of assets. In this sense, joint techniques and basic tools are required to guarantee a correct understanding and implementation of the process of transformation, as shown in Figure 15.

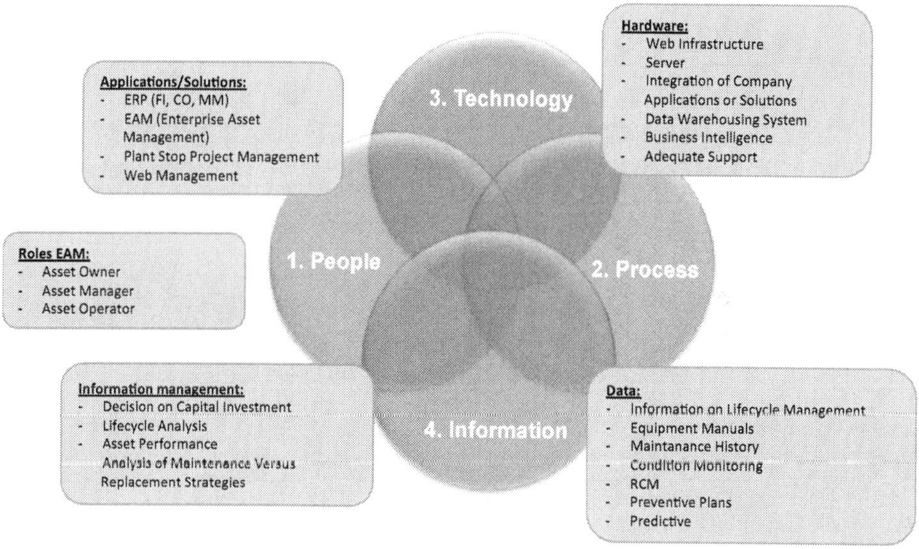

Figure 15: Critical integration factors for success *(Amendola, 2011)*

The minimum tools required are:

- **Processes manual:** A document that describes how core asset management processes and existing interrelationships should be, not only within maintenance management, but between it and the organization's divisions, clients and suppliers, such as operations, human resources, materials, engineering, finances, etc.

- **Organization design:** Development of competencies based on the adoption of ISO 55001, where the structure of the organization, the roles, personnel profiles, career plans, etc., are contemplated.
- **Diagnostic tools:** To evaluate how physical asset management in the organization is being carried out. Through these tools, you can measure: the degree of evolution of maintenance and operations management, production, the alignment and coordination of the rest of the areas with the business and whether the company can really demonstrate that it is generating value. As a result of these tools, each asset, process, or system can be placed on the evolution of the processes road map and, therefore, define specific actions of evolution.
- **System of measurement:** A collection of necessary information and calculation of strategic, operative and tactic management indices in technical areas. These management and financial areas must be constantly monitored to follow up on and define the correlations between them and the progress of the organization's maturity level.

Good Practices

Having a model for asset management creates a way of operating in a document with the support of technology. This makes the management itself tangible and allows it to be put into practice in a more organized way. The management, direction style and principal value of integral physical asset management should be organized in such a way to avoid misguiding the focus of your management to the chaos of the various day-to-day needs. In other words, it provides guidance, organization and a sense of importance.

Even though a management model gives you a sense of order and clarity, not many organizations have the resources or the structure for it. They can only take some of the key processes and structure their own management model. It's worth mentioning that having some form of a model is recommended to give the organization order and structure.

Finally, once the model has been created, the most important thing is to articulate it. This task, led by the asset manager, must be accompanied by an adequate communications and dissemination strategy, as well as clear responsibilities defined in each part of the model.

Designing an Asset Maintenance Maturity Model

A conceptual model of an asset maintenance maturity model (AMMM) can be created under a maintenance process maturity (MPM) framework. It enumerates management objectives and respective performance measures derived from reviewing literature and validated by studies of industrial cases. The model has the ability to approach deficiencies associated with the MPM framework, including:

- Describing the list of possible maintenance objectives, as well as maintenance performance indicators.
- Explicitly linking maintenance performance indicators (MPI) with the objectives of maintenance.
- Identifying and mitigating the failures of different measures of maintenance performance as a function of work and business contexts.

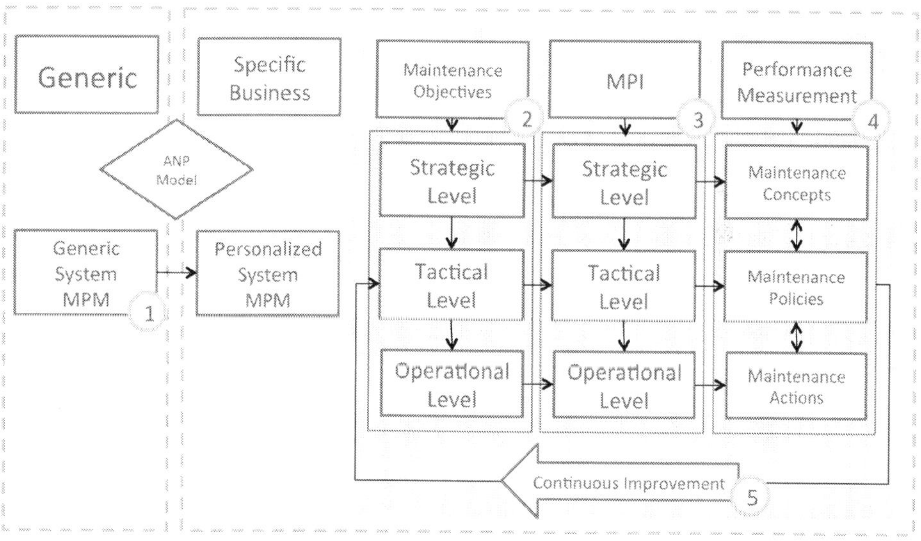

Figure 16: Maintenance performance measurement (MPM) framework *(Adapted from Van Horenbeek, 2014)*

The MPM model shown in Figure 16 explicitly links the different measures of maintenance performance to all levels of the organization. It takes into account the importance of maintenance variables, maintenance objectives and respective indicators. The model consists of five steps:

1. Turn a generic MPM framework into a personalized MPM system, taking into account all levels of the organization.
2. Give maintenance objectives priority in all levels of the organization on the basis of the analytical network process methodology.
3. Make the maintenance performance measures specific to the business with MPIs.
4. Measure, control and monitor maintenance yield based on MPIs.
5. Search for continual improvement by redefining maintenance objectives according to the evolution of the business (i.e., performance measurement and comparative evaluation).

The AMMM is comprised of three phases that include yield evaluation, continual improvement, and comparative evaluation and normalization (Figure 17).

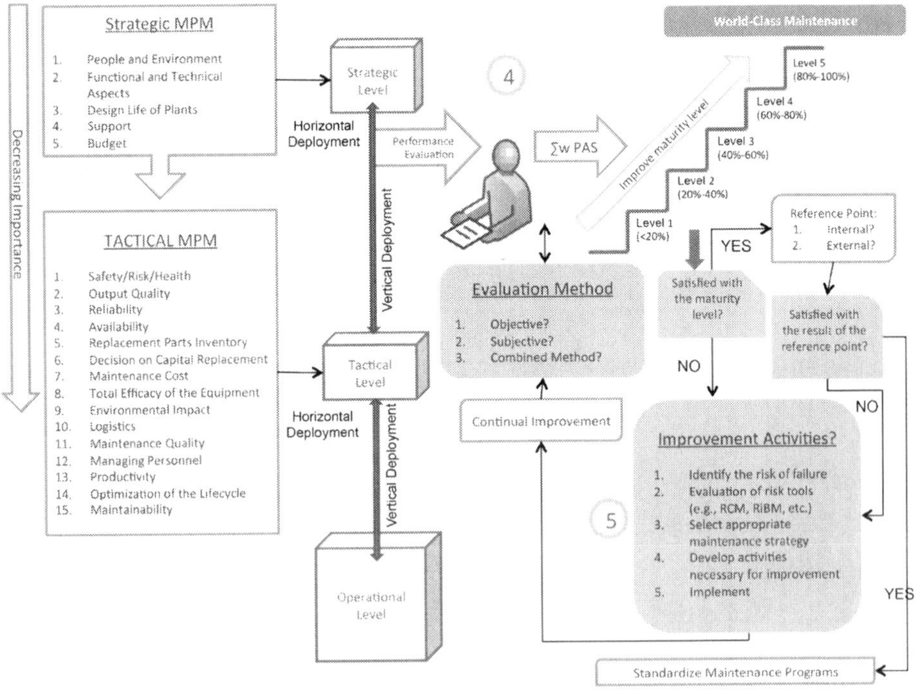

Figure 17: Proposal of an asset management maturity model (AMMM) framework *(Adapted from Van Horenbeek, 2014)*

Purpose of the AMMM's Asset Management Council

The purpose of the AMMM is to present the basic way of thinking for asset management and document the fundamental base of asset management. The intention of the model is to serve as a conceptual framework from which the fundamental elements of asset management can be identified, documented and implemented.

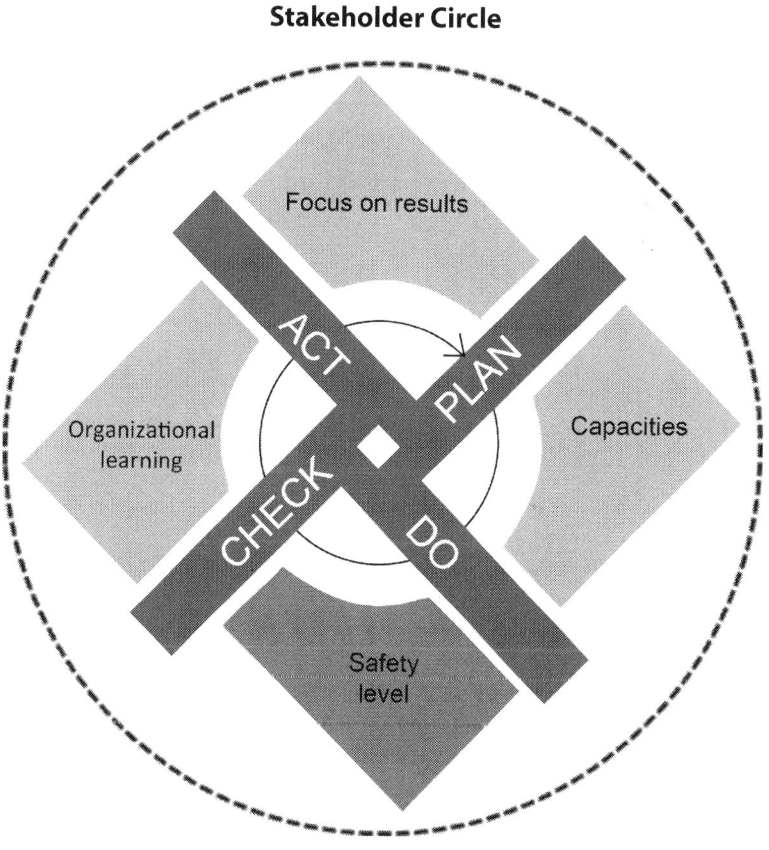

Figure 18: Asset Management Council's asset capability concept model

The AMMM Concept

The AMMM consists of four key principles connected in a set of processes within which the plan-do-check-act focus is implemented. These are enveloped by a stakeholder circle or a circle of interested parties as shown in Figure 19. The interested parties are represented conceptually as those who span and influence all activities.

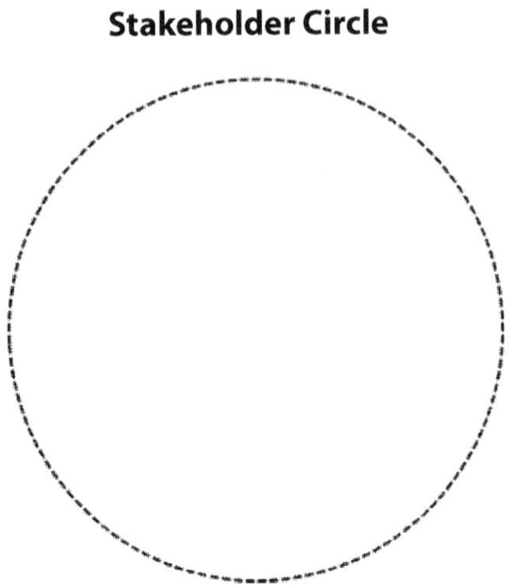

Figure 19: Stakeholder circle, Asset Management Council

Principles

The second part of the AMMM concept are the principles of asset management.

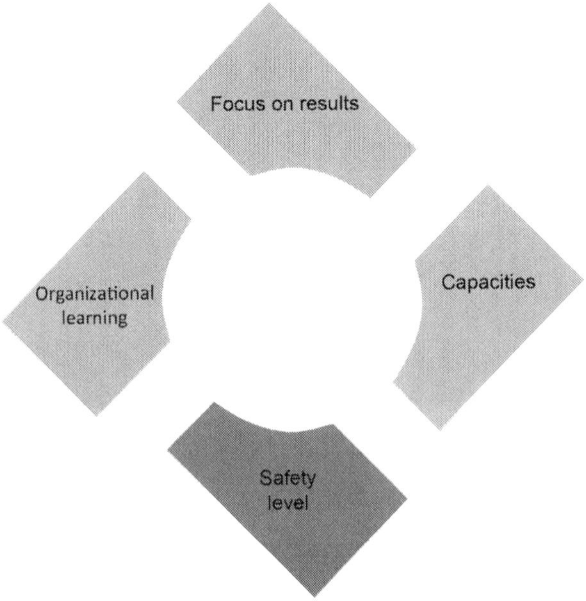

Figure 20: Four principles of the Asset Management Council's asset capability concept model

The four principles of asset management are:

1. Focus on outputs;
2. Capacities;
3. Safety level;
4. Learning organization.

1. Focus on outputs

The first fundamental principle of asset management is for an organization and its assets to have a focus on outputs (i.e., results). This focus must be compatible with the organization's objectives, as described in policies, strategies and plans agreed to by asset management. These business objectives are generally defined in external agreements that the organization has committed to honoring. Lastly, these outputs can be defined in a variety of ways, with each measured in a concerted way so it is clear that the output or service has effectively been provided.

2. Capacities

Capacities are inherent to both organizations and assets. In order to achieve outputs, capacities are needed. Asset management is not about the physical asset itself, but rather the asset generating value through its capacities.

Achieving the required output needs not only the required asset capacities, but also other enabling capacities, like instructions for use, maintenance and replacement parts. These support capacities are enabled by other support capacities, such as finances, human resources, information technology and company outlook.

Example of capacity: A pen is not always necessary to write. Its necessary capacities depend on what one needs to do. If that use is as a paperweight, then the ink in the pen is more important, due to its weight, than the clarity of the tip and the force of its structure. Objects can have many capacities.

Establishing the need to enable capacities is fundamental to linking them to the intentioned output within the operative context. Therefore, the maintenance task of an original equipment manufacturer (OEM) can be of little value if the context of use of the asset isn't known or is significantly different from its original context of use.

3. Safety level

The third key is the assurance level or the uncertainty level. In other words, what is the level of confidence that the asset will reach the predicted or designed results regarding safety, service and profitability? This includes its certainty and its uncertainty.

Risk is the combination of the probability or possibility of an event and its consequence. For example, the consequence in the majority of aviation accidents is death. Yet, people fly in planes because they feel certain the plane will perform at the expected safety level. People are sure of that safety because of the way in which risk is managed through the use of evaluation tools during design and later in the presentation of support and enabling capacities.

The management of risk is a key function of asset management. It provides a level of assurance, in that the systems and equipment that are part of the asset will deliver measurable and verifiable capacities. Therefore, the concept of assurance level is really incorporated in the concept of output.

Organizations that are good at asset management effectively manage the what would happen if scenarios that imply a compromise between the level of confidence and the consequence. That's because they are able to connect actions with consequences.

Example of a level of assurance: A railway system of interurban passengers, with its existing asset configuration and the associated regimes of operations and maintenance management, is able to produce the hourly yield required for each train, with a ninety-two percent probability at a determined cost. Here, ninety-two percent relates to the level of assurance or confidence that ninety-two percent of trains selected at random will arrive at their destination on time.

4. Learning Organization

The fourth key principle of asset management is the learning organization, where the lessons are gathered through the measurement and analysis of yield. Therefore, learning is disseminated and acted on. An organization that actively seeks change in the environment or has a firm grasp on knowledge and adapts to improve its products or services is a learning organization.

So, the question is: If you only need eighty percent of the execution time, what would the cost be? What would you do differently to manage this asset and what would the difference in cost be?

For example, the difference between a seventy-five percent level of confidence and ninety-nine percent confidence is a two hundred and fifty to one ratio, meaning that if the ninety-nine percent represents one failure a month, then seventy-five percent represents two hundred and fifty failures a month, clearly affecting the provision of resources.

Evidently, organizations that manage assets well are learning organizations. They have process transparency and transparency in related decision-making. Their focus can be considered a vision of continual improvement that centers on people, the understanding of their roles in the organization, its capacity to see processes and foreseen resources, and its capacity to challenge the regime and not feel threatened.

Plan-Do-Check-Act: A Process

Asset management is a process, a series of steps and/or actions that allow the performance of a function or achievement of a result. As such, there's a beginning and an end. In the middle are feedback cycles to continuously maintain the alignment between the administered assets and the interest groups that are tended to and affected by the asset.

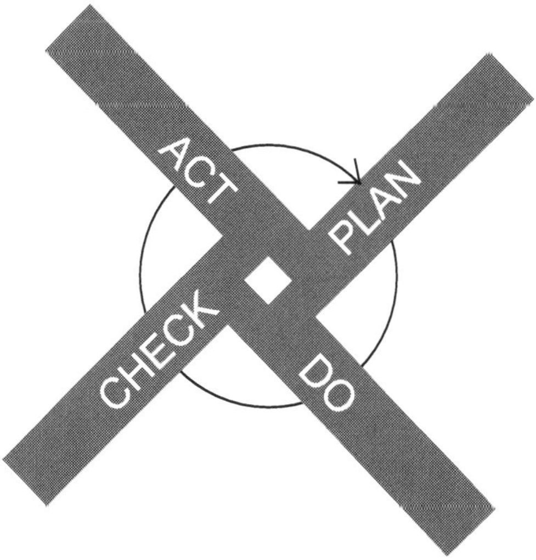

Figure 21: Asset Management Council's plan, do, check, act model

The process follows the classical model, plan-do-check-act, originally defined by Walter A. Shewhart more than fifty years ago.

Application of the Capacity Model

When implementing an asset management system, an organization has to choose appropriately:

- Technical, financial, company and convention processes;
- Organizational roles, structures and competencies;
- Technical, financial and operative plans;
- Decision-making plans based on risk.

The capacity model schematically presents the processes that can be used partially or completely to obtain the products determined by the organization.

The processes are found in six major disciplines:

1. Management of demand;
2. Engineering systems;
3. Management of configuration;
4. Acquisitions;
5. Operations and maintenance;
6. Continual improvement.

These disciplines are associated with a number of national and international standards, such as ISO/IEC 15288 systems engineering. This technical specification seeks to provide a brief introduction to both asset management and the requisites for an asset management system.

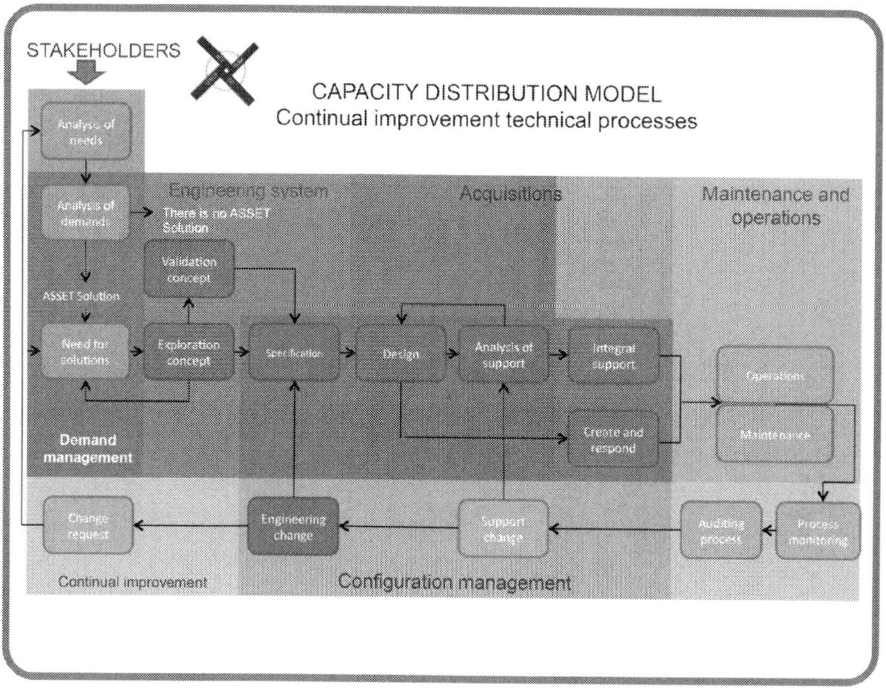

Figure 22: Capacity distribution model, Asset Management Council

Asset Management System and Organizational System Model

A system of management is the set of interrelated elements of an organization that interact to establish policies, objectives and processes to reach the organization's objectives. An asset management system can approach a single discipline or several, as illustrated in Figure 23.

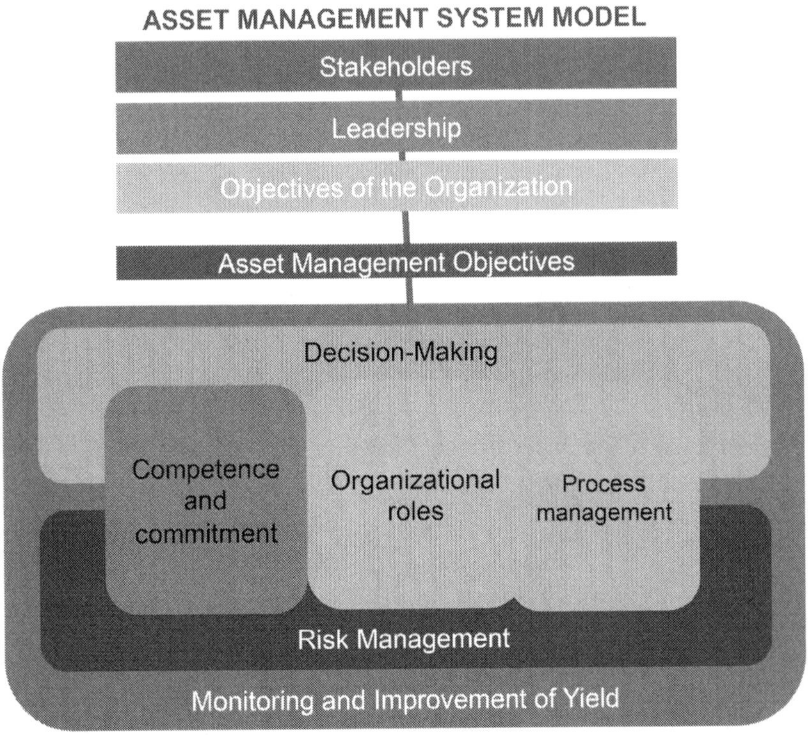

Figure 23: Asset management system model, Asset Management Council

In small organizations, it's possible there isn't a formal, documented system. However, the larger the organization, the more likely it is for written instructions about policies and processes to exist. This assures that nothing is omitted and that everyone is clear about who should do what, when and how.

The asset management system model defines the parts of a management system for asset management and the relationship among these parts.

Apart from defining these relationships, the asset management system model describes the links between the needs of the interested parties, the directive, the culture, the organization's objectives and the objectives of the asset management.

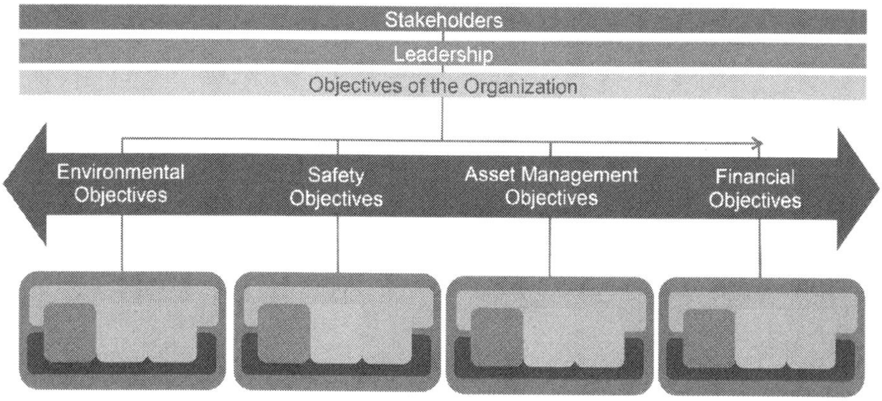

Figure 24: Organizational system model, Asset Management Council

The organizational system model in Figure 24 illustrates the interrelationship among the different management systems of the organization. The asset management system model illustrates the key elements of the asset management system and how they interrelate. It also illustrates the typical components of the organization's management system and how they interrelate.

These models are presented together. One is embedded in the other: the asset management system model is a system within the organizational system model.

Conceptual Model of Physical Asset Management

The Institute of Asset Management (IAM) worked with international partners from the Global Forum on Maintenance and Asset Management (GFMAM) to reach a consensus on the definition of a model. The purpose was to develop a common focus of the qualifications associated with asset management, directed at settling and aligning knowledge. In this sense, the topics of asset management are linked to six groups that form the conceptual model for physical asset management, as shown in Figure 25.

Asset Management Model

This section shows how to transform these principles into actions through the use of the management model concept. This requires moving efforts and resources in a single direction in order to achieve the proposed objectives of improving physical asset management and associating these with good practices.

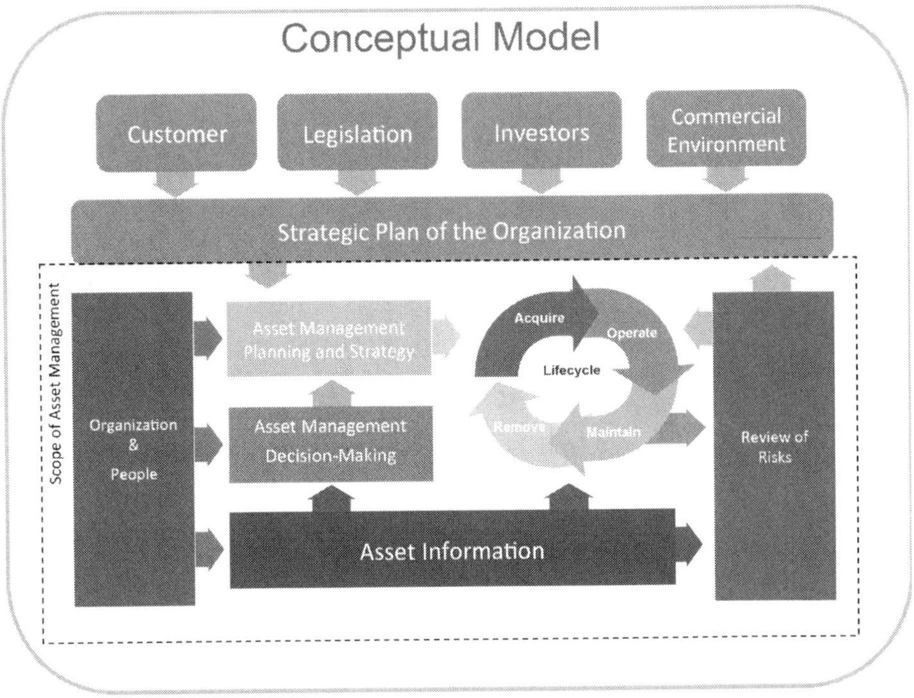

Figure 25: Physical asset management conceptual model, Institute of Asset Management

First, it's important to understand what a management model is. To begin, a model refers to a graphic or idealized representation that supports the organization with a reality of a system. This makes it possible to interact with its components.

An organized system can be modeled in multiple ways, so it's necessary to focus attention on the way in which the organizational components respond in order to implement the right model. The proper model itself is supported by theory and asset management practices so it can achieve the desired results. These results are later used to compare and contrast with current reality to refine the actions that need to be taken in the execution phase.

Therefore, a model represents the function and order of a determined system. It represents how you integrate the different elements that form a part of the system for adequate implementation of physical asset management.

In Figure 26, a real example of a management model associated with integral physical asset management is shown. In its interpretation, elements that operate in the system are observed: a projects stage (CAPEX), an operations and maintenance stage (OPEX), technical/financial indicators and a reliability strategies (operational) stage. They are all immersed in an environment of asset management policies, competency development, process safety management (PSM), management of change (MOC), environmental, social corporate responsibility and the business plan.

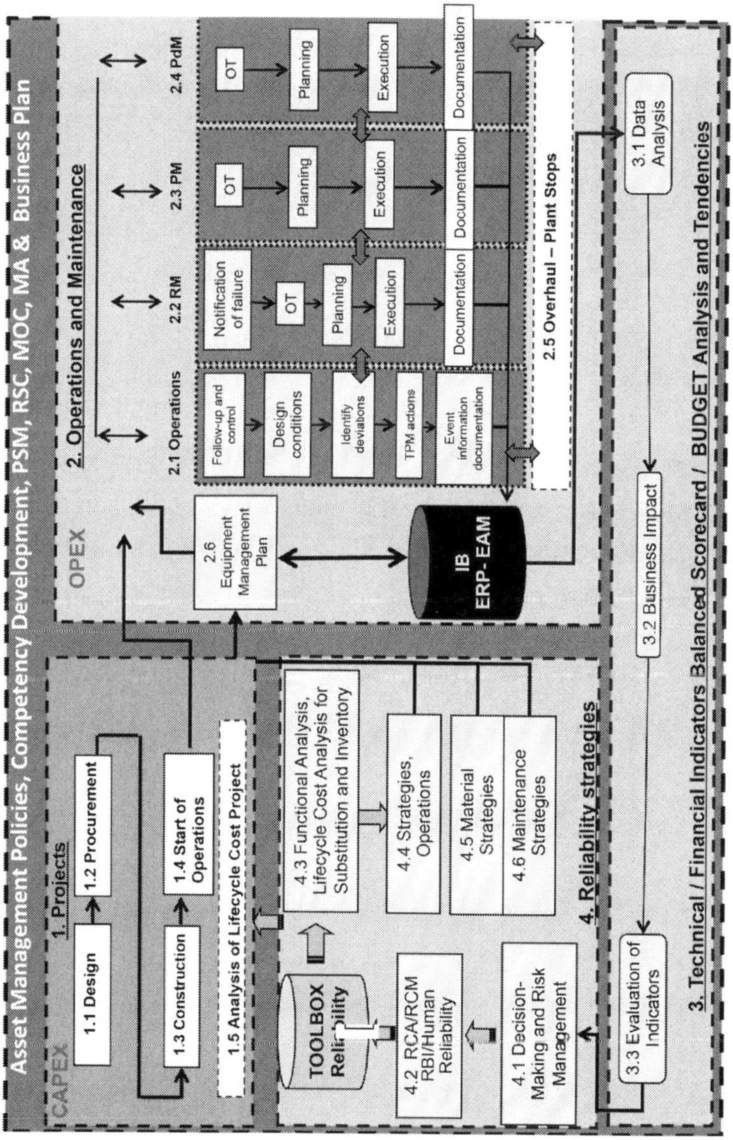

Figure 26: Integral asset management model *(Amendola, L., 2006, 2011, 2013, 2014, 2016 Copyright PMM)*

Additionally, Figure 26 shows that the elements of the system interact among themselves, receiving, processing and producing information, or feeding continuously. Each element, itself, serves some internal process that must be executed. Starting from a similar model, you, too, can transform reality and manage to achieve concrete results.

Figure 26 further illustrates that the center of actions is the implementation of the physical asset management model, with the objective of finding the plant or asset that operates at one hundred percent of its productive design capability, eliminating losses and, in that way, increasing efficiency of the operation. It's here where the concept of maintenance directed solely by the actions of repairing or being limited to preventive maintenance actions has ceased to be valid.

Asset management is a business that extends to assuring asset reliability through concrete actions linked to good practices and referenced under a management model through which the way of doing things is defined so it can be measured and audited (i.e., focused on continual improvement).

In each of these implementation stages of the asset management model, important obstacles exist that frequently prevent achieving the potential results of an effective process of strategic management of physical assets. Some obstacles to consider are:

- Regarding design, how do you manage a valid and useful strategy both in the short and long term? How can you challenge your vision, discover new competitive spaces and drive to innovate?
- Concerning deployment, what are the best ways and optimal sequence to communicate the strategy or stages? What should the strategic information system be and how should it be implemented?
- At this stage, many implementations of asset management fail, given that the proposed answers to the questions tend to be generic or reflect interests that run parallel to the strategic management of asset management (ISO 55001).

In particular, it's important to recognize that the deployment of a strategy that is aligned with the strategic asset management plan (SAMP) is aligned with ISO 55001. This is a topic that is not only structural, but one that should be adapted to unique conditions of each company, such as its organization and management culture, as well as the specific content of its strategy.

QUESTION: In industry, how do you manage, for example, to have culture and organizational capacities directly support the achievement of strategic results of the integral asset management model?

POSSIBLE ANSWER: By working with people from the base to the directors. In other words, by connecting the floor of the plant (tactic) with the castle (strategic).

Figure 27 shows a framework for sustainable asset management. The three levels are: execution; tactics, where strategies are implemented; and strategic plan, where actions are prioritized.

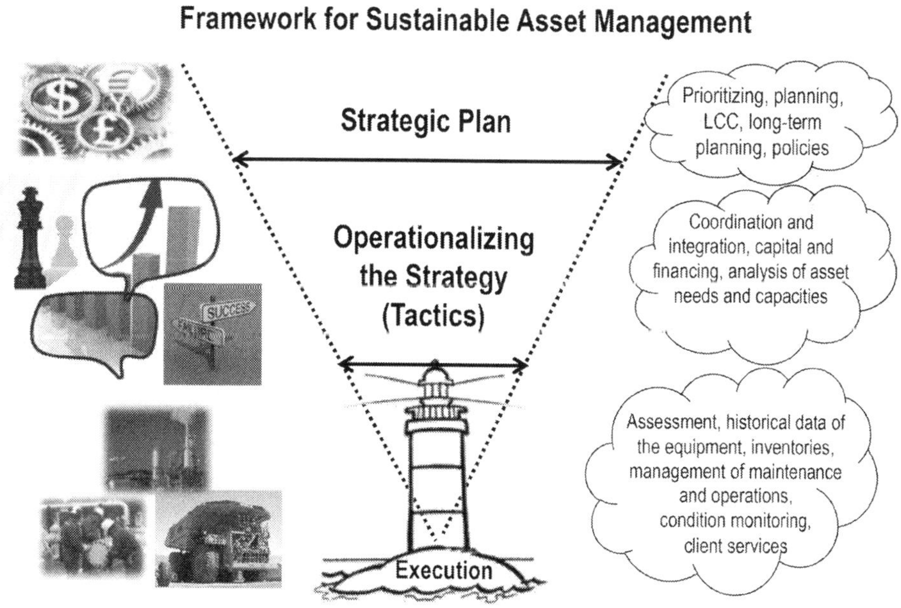

Figure 27: Framework for sustainable asset management *(Amendola, L., Depool, T., 2012)*

Consider these questions:

- How can you promote an effective process of strategic management?
- What cultural and leadership characteristics are key and how do you ensure they proliferate?
- How do you assure a transition that delivers results in the short and long term?
- How do you focus the organization on initiatives that are priorities for strategy?

Without a doubt, the core component for achieving an organization's transformation is executive commitment and leadership. Considering this statement, the basic components of the asset management model are:

a. A chain of cause and effect relationships that express the set of hypotheses of the strategy through the strategic objectives and their achievement through performance indicators.

b. A link to financial and technical results of the business, business objectives and their respective indicators to reflect the systemic composition of the strategy through the four perspectives of the management of assets defined in ISO 55001: human assets, financial assets, information assets and intangible assets. Finally, you must translate results into financial achievements that bring about the maximization of value created by the business to its shareholders.

c. Key indicators of results and guide indicators that are separate from indicators that reflect the final performance of the business and technical indicators. These sets of indicators are designed to reflect things that need to be done well in order to achieve an objective and measure progress of the actions that bring you closer to the achievement of the objective. The purpose is to channel actions and efforts to the business strategy.

d. Measurements that generate and drive change to motivate certain kinds of behaviors associated both with achievement and the communication of organizational, team and individual results. This fundamental component defines indicators that generate the expected behaviors, particularly those that guide the organization to adaptability in the face of an environment of permanent and accelerated change.

e. Aligning initiatives or projects with strategy through strategic objectives. Each project that exists in the company must be directly linked with the leverage of expected achievements for the diverse objectives and indicators.

f. Consensus among the management team of the company or organization begins with the asset management model and a dialogue between the members of the management team to achieve the business strategy and provide an agreement on how to measure and support that which is important to the achievement of the strategy.

Clover Model of Asset Integrity Management

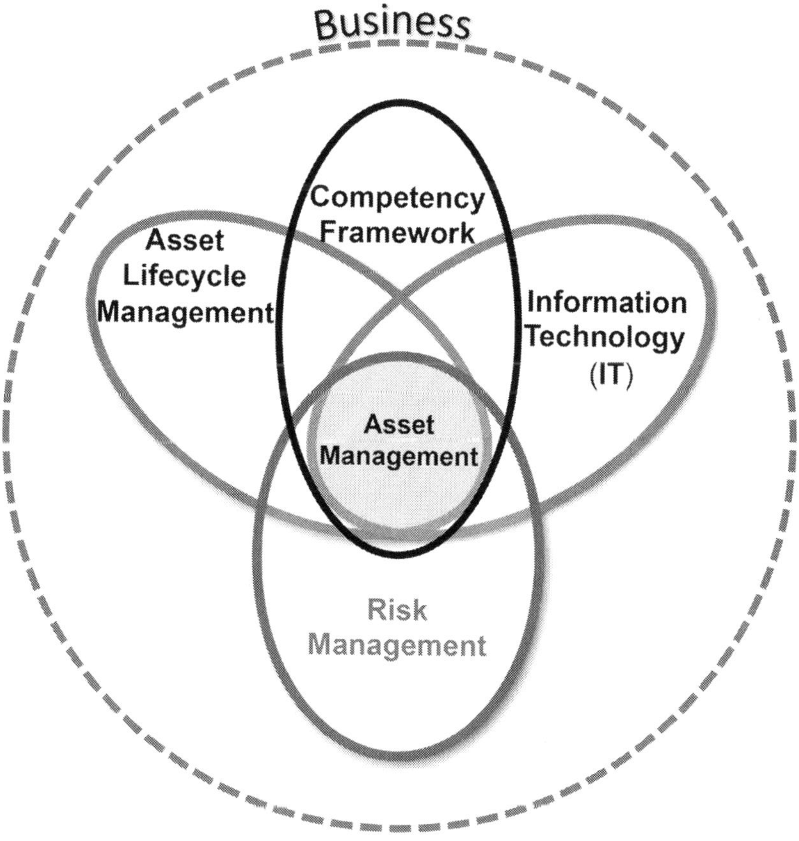

Figure 28: Clover asset integrity management model *(Amendola, L., 2015)*

The clover model seeks to strengthen key corporate activities, abandoning nonessential or peripheral functions. In this model, asset management is the nucleus and around its axis are four pillars or leaves that correspond with four types of strategies.

1. **In the first leaf, the competency framework nucleus can be found.** This is where all activities that are unique to the human talent of the company can be found. It's composed of a set of professionals at the strategic, tactical and operative level that have essential importance to the company and qualified workers with a high level of knowledge on the key competencies of the organization.
2. **The second leaf is information technology (IT)**, the set of resources, procedures and techniques used in the processing, warehousing and transmission of information. IT has blended into computer information technology (CIT), as currently, it isn't enough talking about a computer when referring to the processing of information. The Internet may form a part of this processing, which can be done in a distributed and remote way. When talking about remote processing, apart from incorporating the concept of telecommunications, one can be referring to a device that is very different from what is traditionally understood to be a computer. For example, devices like a mobile phone, tablet, or laptop computer, can be carried out of the workplace and have the capacity to operate on the Web via wireless communications, with more features, ease and performance.
3. **The third clover leaf corresponds to risk management**, which is a structured focus for managing uncertainty relative to a threat through a sequence of human activities that include risk evaluation, the development strategies to manage it and mitigation using management resources. The strategies include transferring risk to other places, evading it, reducing its negative effects and accepting some or all of the consequences of a particular risk.
4. **The fourth leaf corresponds to the price of the asset's lifecycle.** It's defined as the cost of the original design in the concept phase, the detailed engineering, construction and installation, plus the

total cost of the property, including operative and maintenance costs, as well as compensation at the end of an asset's life. The analysis of the asset's lifecycle cost (LCC) determines the net present value (NPV) of the asset engineering decisions to select new assets and/or establish an asset management system.

Encircling the clover is the business plan, a representation of the model to be followed. It brings together information on what the business is or will be. It's also considered a synthesis of how the owner of the business, the administrator, or businessperson will try to organize company labor and carry out the activities necessary and sufficient for success.

Deconstructed Clover Asset Integrity Management Model

The parts of the model are shown in Figures 29 to 33.

Figure 29: Risk Management Model *(Amendola, L., 2007)*

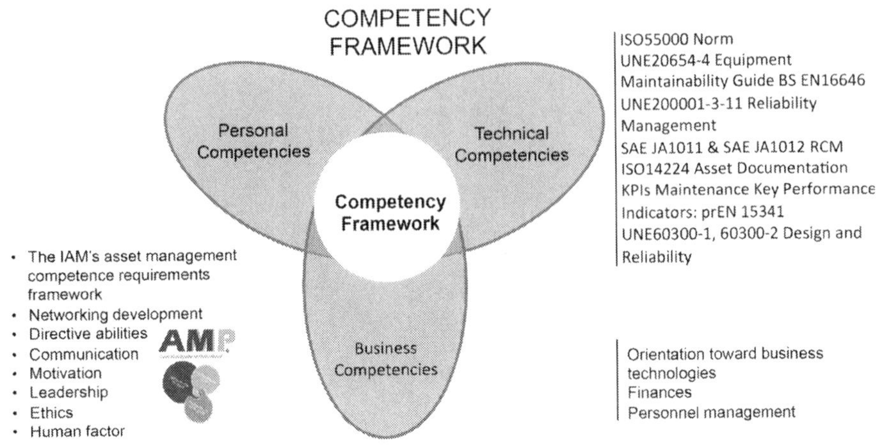

Figure 30: Asset Manager Professional (AMP) competency framework *(Brand 2.897.506 Patent and Brands Office, Spain; Amendola, L., 2009)*

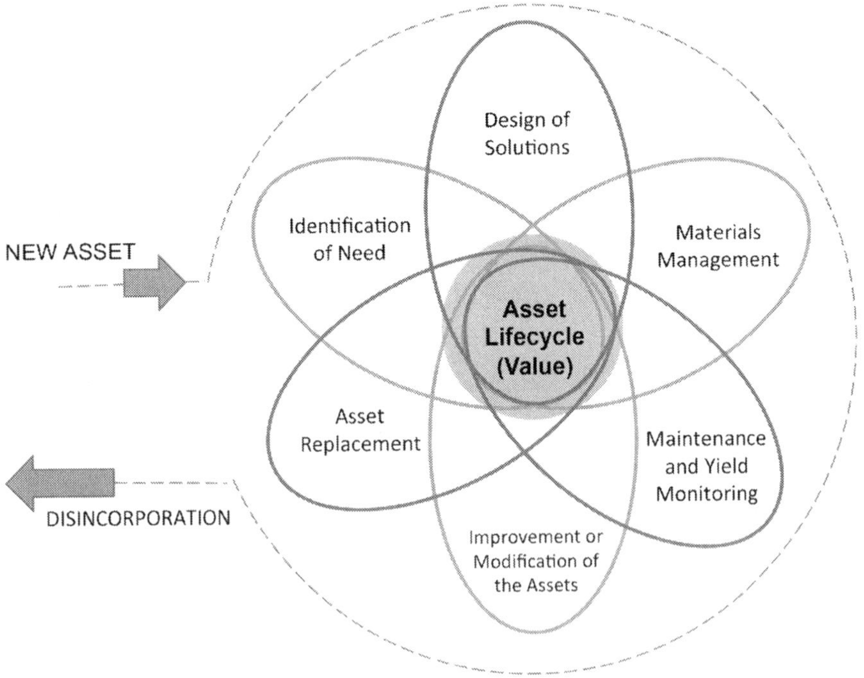

Figure 31: Asset integrity management model *(Amendola. L., 2015)*

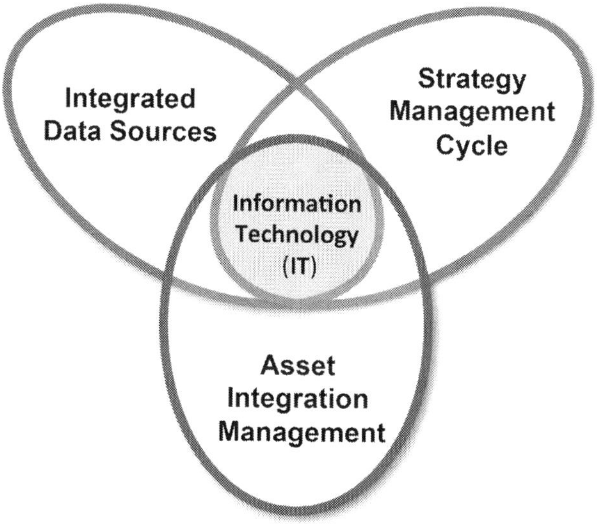

Figure 32: Information technology model (Amendola, L., 2007)

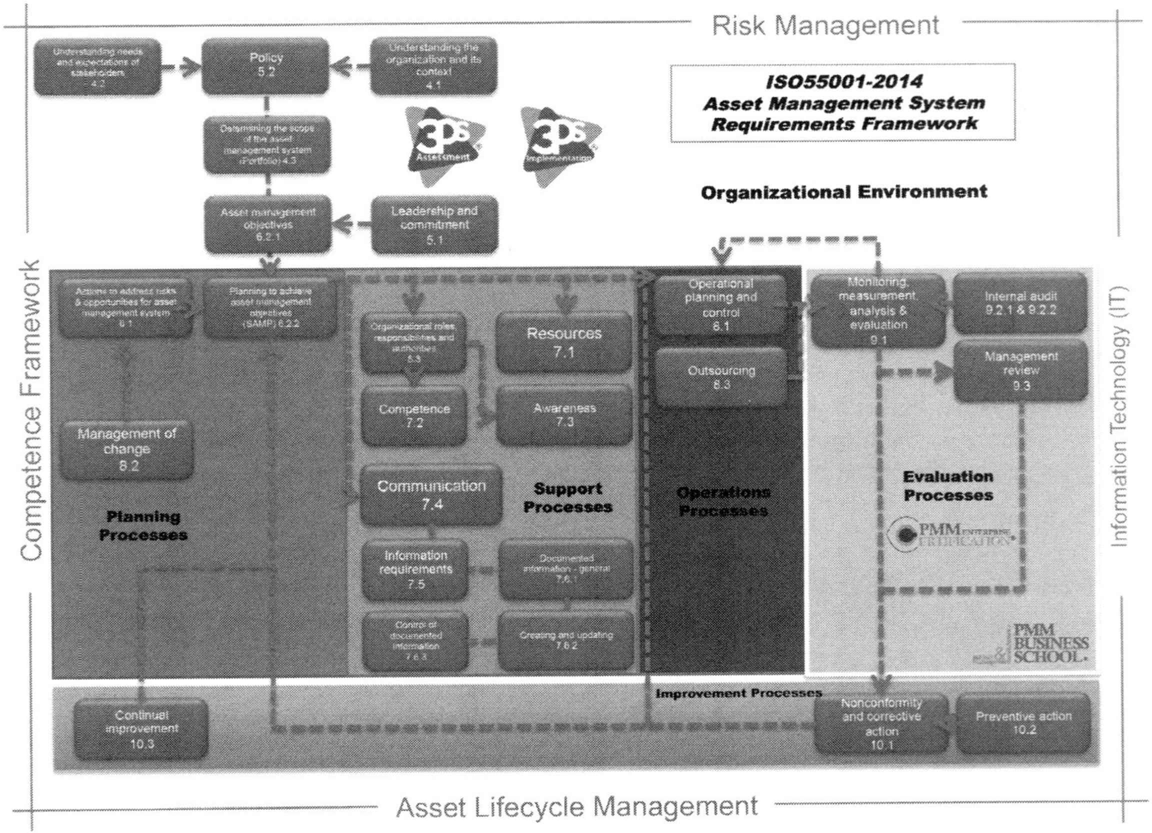

Figure 33: Aligned clover asset integrity management model, ISO55001

Chef's Recommendations:

The design of a model isn't just copy and paste; it's a serious process that will help to fertilize the ground. A model must not stay in theory, but contribute to structure and organization, and be the framework of reference for defining tools and techniques to be employed, performance indicators, etc. It's important to design the PLATE well, as much as making sure the food is TASTY.

MANAGEMENT OF CHANGE (MOC)

The Importance of the Human Factor in Achieving Success in the Change Process

In today's world, both public and private companies must confront the political, economic, social and cultural environment of constant change, where the power of the human factor leads the transition to change and its implementation within the organization.

Only one thing seems true: The only thing that stays constant is change. What is change? The Royal Spanish Academy of Language defines it as "action and effect of changing." This definition must not allow you to forget that you need to understand every change not as a single event, restricted in time, but, on the contrary, as a continual process, slow, interactive and multifactorial.

Using History to Understand the Present and Model the Future

In 1983, a team from Shell studied the long-term survival of companies. They searched for companies that existed from the last quarter of the nineteenth century, that is, more than one hundred years old. The companies also needed to be important within their sector and have a strong corporate identity.

The team found thirty companies in North America, Europe and Japan between one hundred and seven hundred years old. Of those, twenty-seven were reasonably well-documented. Some of them are DuPont, Grace, Mitsui, Sumitomo and Siemens.

The first conclusion that can be drawn is that the average life of the corporations is shorter than its potential life. A study by Fortune 500 confirms that the average life of companies is less than fifty years, whereas their life expectancy rises to one hundred years.

The second observation of the Shell study, and the one that is most interesting for this book's topic, is that those companies are very good with regard to directing change.

The history worldwide has helped the industry evolve to what it is today. For most of its life, it depended on messengers, horsemen and ships to deliver messages and now, in current times, phones, planes and electronic webs. The business portfolio has changed continuously, from copper to forestry, from the melting of steel to hydropower to now making paper, pulp and chemical products. Its production and technology have changed through time, from steam to internal combustion, to electricity, to microchips. The history continues to adapt itself to the world of continuous change.

From all of this, it's important to note how important it is to learn from those organizations that have managed to adapt through time to changing environments and successfully survive. The key to management of change and adapting at all times to the needs of the market is gathering flexible personnel who share the proactive nature of the organization's strategy, commits to the company and are capable of adapting to new needs.

When these forces make their appearance, the organization can opt to ignore them, or analyze them and react or implement change within itself and survive.

Effectively facing the challenge of change is necessary, even if only for a single reason: survival.

The result of ignoring change and preserving traditional customs as the way of doing and thinking about things leads to stagnation, decadency and failure. That's why one must effectively face the challenge of change in order to survive.

If the decision is to face change, it can be treated in two ways:

1. **As a reactive process.** In this case, the directive opts for maintaining the organization on a fixed course, solving problems according to how they come up. This barely implies planning of actions, given that the directive itself doesn't consider the change threatening to its existence.
2. **Like a proactive process.** In this case, there are deliberate actions to modify the status quo, given that what is attempted is to anticipate change both from the outside and the inside of the organization and finding ways to successfully come out of the new situation.

In the face of a change that happens to an organization, the reactions – both of the directive and the employees – are very diverse. The most common are:

- Denying that change is taking place;
- Ignoring change with the false hope that problems will disappear on their own over the course of time;
- Proposing resistance to change out of fear, lack of understanding change, etc.;
- Accepting change and adapting to it; conceiving it as a new way of life;
- Anticipating the change and planning for it, like the companies that achieve the most progress do.

The Concept of Human Capital

North American economist Gary Becker was awarded the Nobel Prize for working on the concept of human capital. However, for a long time, his work was ignored and criticized by major economists around the world who didn't consider him a true economist because of his dedication to studying such a concept, extending the microeconomical domain to a broad range of human behavior and interaction (Figure 34).

Figure 34: Human factor interaction

Becker began to study knowledge societies and concluded in his study that the biggest treasure was the human capital they had, that is, the knowledge and abilities that form a part of people, their health and the quality of their work habits. Additionally, he defines human capital as important for the productivity of modern economies, given that this productivity is based on creation, dissemination and use of knowledge.

Knowledge is created in companies, laboratories and universities. It is disseminated by way of families, education centers and workplaces and used to produce goods and services. Whereas previously, economic development was considered the priority and everything else, like education, housing and health would follow, today, it's completely different, given that the link between education and economic progress is essential.

Becker points this out in this way: "The importance of human capital can be seen from the experiences of workers in modern economies that lack sufficient education and training in the workplace."

Why Development Management by Competencies Is Necessary

Management by competencies is one of the major tools in the development of human capital. It marks the difference between a course for skill development and a structure that encompasses skill development, training and the experience necessary to define job requirements or identify the capacities of a worker or professional.

Therefore, it's important to validate more knowledge or operational experience by making it more comprehensible and acceptable to all workers in the company.

A critical topic the model addresses is the promotion of innovation for technological leadership. Workers will know their competency profile and the one required for the place they occupy or aspire to occupy, identifying and acting on the necessary actions in order to have the required profile. In this way, an atmosphere for innovation is promoted from the base, fundamentally through self-development.

All this deepens the strategic company-worker alliance by generating better HR with career development, mobility, flexibility and better employability.

Integration of the Human System

A preventive culture in a company would not be complete if an acceptable level of integration of the human system didn't exist. Indeed, this implies the integration of the entire organization, with all its functions in a state of permanent perfection.

A business organization cannot exist with elevated levels of efficiency if there isn't an elevated level of integration of a preventive culture. So, if prevention isn't present in all areas and at all hierarchical levels, you could hardly count on reliability management and management of the risks of tangible and intangible assets.

In modern companies, these require engineering the human factor as adequate tools in times of technical innovation. The goal is to guarantee competitive advantage and effective practices of adequate and permanent information that manage to effectively link higher management and the operators. With this purpose, the human factor acquires more importance and resources like skill building and technical updating of the human resources in the operation realm.

The organizing idea is cultural transformation, as it urges a rethinking of the relationship between management and the levels in charge of productive operations, and the integration of communications to marketing and the relationship that originates between the organization and its public image, the clients and the market in general.

The integration of human systems is of higher importance, from the point in which a tacit commitment is formed. It's about constructing long-term relationships with employees and establishing alternative methods that favor reputation and credibility. Effectiveness of company communications can be achieved only when employee loyalty is secured.

Communications is everything in a company, including all areas relative to contact with the public. Although outward communications is indispensable, without good internal communications, the former would be more difficult. The latter tries to put all work areas of the company in contact with each other. This is apart from attempting to favor work relations, instilling the feeling of permanency of a worker with its company, recognition as a collaborator and ensuring human and material resources to the safety of personnel.

The integration of the human system model shown in Figure 35 offers guidance for obtaining fluidity in communications and contact with all human development within an organization. From the outset, skill building and managing human talent with regard to transmitting its ideas, concepts and knowledge to achieve the correct and safe way of working will guarantee that workers have the mechanisms to inform on risks in facilities, the procedures to work safely, correct tool use and all risks associated with the facility.

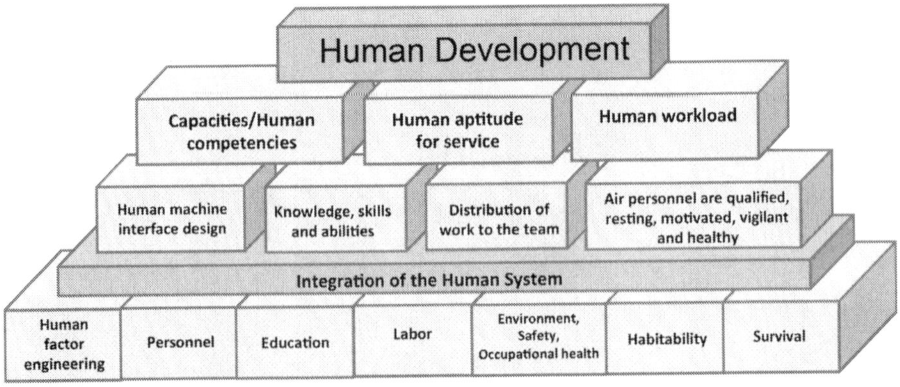

Figure 35: Human factor interaction

Contact is the organization's capacity to manage with special intelligence the personal direction it must express to each and every one of its employees.

Management of Change (MOC)

Managing process changes during the life of a facility is one of the twenty-three requirements of ISO 55000, 8.2 Management of Change, and subsection ii is part of the elements of Implementation of Asset Management Plans – Activities of the Lifecycle and Performance Evaluation and Improvements. The management practices that apply are:

1. The recognition of situations of change;
2. Risk evaluation;
3. Decisions on whether or not to allow change;
4. Control of the necessary risks and follow-up on measures.

According to point 8.2.1 under ISO 55001 Requirement 8.2 – Management of Change, "internal or external changes that affect assets, the management of assets, or the system for asset management can impact the organization's aptitude to achieve its asset management objectives. In this sense, such changes should be analyzed and measures should be taken to mitigate them before their implementation. The organization should review the consequences associated with the changes, both planned and unplanned, and take necessary actions to mitigate any unpredicted adverse effect."

According to point 8.2.2, "the organization's considerations should approach changes that include, but are not limited to:

a. Organizational structures, roles, or responsibilities;
b. Asset management policy, objectives, or plans;
c. Processes and procedures of asset management activities;
d. New assets, asset systems, or technologies, including obsolescence;
e. Factors external to the organization, including new legal or regulatory requisites;
f. Restrictions in the supply chain;
g. Demands for products and services, contractors, or suppliers;
h. Demands for resources, including competitive demands.

According to point 8.2.3, "the organization should have the capacity to make decisions based on evidence on the proposed changes and the aptitude to consider scenarios systematically within the whole organization."

The risks associated with change should be considered with regard to its impacts on asset management and the asset management system. This should include the involuntary consequences to other parts of the organization as a result of change, for example, the impact of resource restrictions due to changes in the requisites in the provision of services.

What Is MOC?

MOC helps assure that changes in a process don't inadvertently introduce new, unpredicted dangers or, without knowing it, increase the risk to employees, the public, or the environment of existing dangers. It does this through a review and authorization process to evaluate the proposed adjustments to facility design, operations, the organization, or activities before implementation.

MOC also includes measures to help make sure personnel who may be impacted are notified of the change and pertinent documents, as well as procedures, knowledge about process safety, etc., are kept updated.

Why MOC Is Important

If a proposal for modification of a dangerous process is made without adequate assessment, the risk of a process safety accident could significantly increase.

When and Where MOC Is Done

MOC assessments are conventionally done in operational plants and are increasingly carried out during the whole lifecycle of the processes within company areas involved in capital project design and planning. MOC assessments should be done in good faith.

Who Performs MOC?

A professional generates a change request (Figure 36). Qualified personnel, normally independent of the change originator, review the request to determine if any potentially adverse impact of risk could result from the change and suggest additional measures to manage risk.

On the basis of the review, the change is authorized for execution, modification, or rejection. Frequently, final approval for implementation of the change comes from another designated person, independent of the review team.

An ample variety of people are usually involved in making the change, notifying or skill building of the potentially affected employees and updating documents affected by the change.

A MOC System

The main product of a MOC system is a request for change that is duly reviewed and authorized, and identifies and assures the implementation of risk controls adequate for the proposed change. It includes adequate revisions and updates with the participation of other practical commercial activities, such as the modification of process safety information, communications and skill building. The outputs of MOC also can be used to ease performance of other elements of commercial practices. An example of a MOC form is shown in Figure 36.

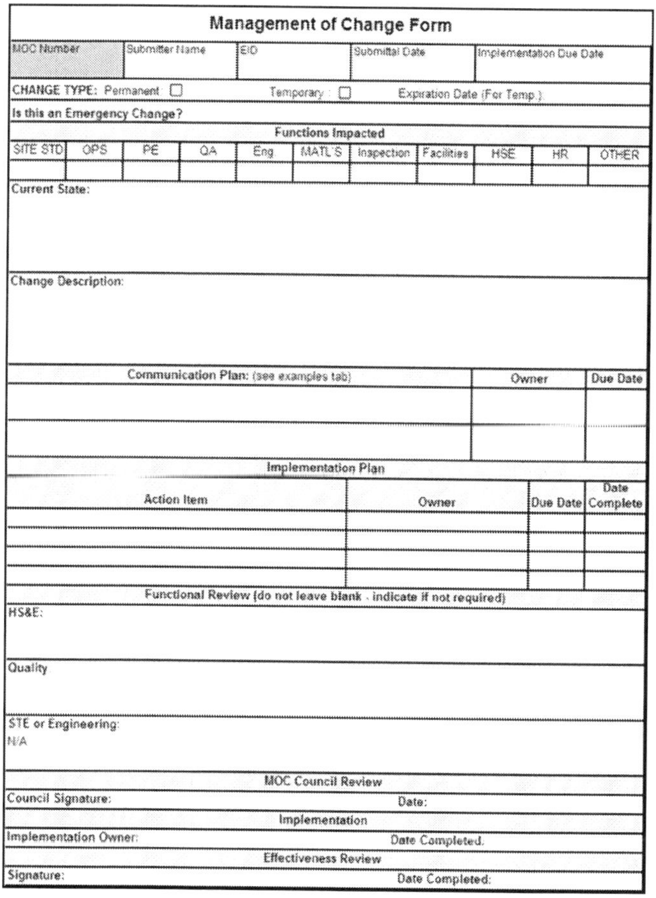

Management of Change Form

MOC Number	Submitter Name	EID	Submittal Date	Implementation Due Date

CHANGE TYPE: Permanent ☐ Temporary ☐ Expiration Date (For Temp.)

Is this an Emergency Change?

Functions Impacted

SITE STD	OPS	PE	QA	Eng	MATL'S	Inspection	Facilities	HSE	HR	OTHER

Current State:

Change Description:

Communication Plan: (see examples tab)	Owner	Due Date

Implementation Plan

Action Item	Owner	Due Date	Date Complete

Functional Review (do not leave blank - indicate if not required)

HS&E:

Quality

STE or Engineering:
N/A

MOC Council Review

Council Signature: Date:

Implementation

Implementation Owner: Date Completed:

Effectiveness Review

Signature: Date Completed:

Figure 36: Management of change (MOC) form example

How MOC Is Done

Organizations generally have written procedures that detail how MOC is implemented. These procedures are applied to all works that present risks.

For this, organizations employ good practices based on the Swiss Cheese model, proposed by James Reason and Dante Orlandella, professors at the University of Manchester. Companies naturally establish barriers to impede external threats. These barriers are constructed within the process and are imagined by Reason and Orlandella as slices of Swiss cheese, with holes that correspond to active or latent errors that exist in any safety system and are constantly opening, closing and changing places.

When these holes are aligned, they materialize risk, doing damage to organizations. Asset managers, with the support of the health, safety and the environment (HSE) team, must evaluate latent errors in the safety system, the design of which can facilitate the entry of infections. This, in turn, generates durable vulnerabilities in the safety system, reflected in poorly conceived procedures and the lack of an adequate design for safety. The latent conditions can be inactive within the system until the combination of active errors by people and critical factors generate the opportunity, leading to the risk materializing.

To better grasp the concept, think of active failures as mosquitoes that can be eliminated one by one, but will continue coming. The best solutions consist of making better defenses that are more effectively based on risk analysis.

For this reason, risk analysis must begin from the understanding of vital company activities, such as policies, action plans, external and internal communications, budgets and controls, and supervision. This is where organizations' risks begin and it's important to contextualize the organization at the start of risk analysis.

- The organization should determine and plan actions, and provide adequate resources to approach the risks of its asset management system. For example, it could incorporate asset management risks within risk registers of divisions and projects, with adequate elevation mechanisms if they are not approachable at the level in which they occur.

- The organization should integrate the identified actions during the implementation plan for the asset management system.
- The organization should be able to demonstrate the way in which it evaluated the actions' effectiveness to manage the identified risks with regard to the organizational objectives and the decision-making criteria.

Asset management seeks a holistic focus. This implies understanding that a hidden face of the organization exists, which is none other than resisting associated threats of operations. With management tools like risk analysis, asset managers seek to make organizations resilient and resistant to the materialization of risk.

Therefore, the worst scenarios must be anticipated and prepared for in the development of organizational activities in order to carry out proper risk analysis.

The Swiss Cheese model in Figure 37 suggests that more obstacles or cheese layers must be placed along the path to risk, which places more mitigation measures, a situation that can be applied to all types of organizations.

The results of the assessment process are often documented in a MOC assessment form. The reference information provided by system designers to help in the assessment process is often attached to the MOC assessment form. Once the change is approved, it is ready for implementation.

Personnel potentially affected are then informed about the change and provided more detailed skill building, as necessary, before the change is put into place.

In addition, activities, such as changes in process safety information and other elements of commercial practices, are evaluated to identify what is required before the change is put into place and what can be postponed until after the start-up. Follow-up is conducted on all these activities until they are completed.

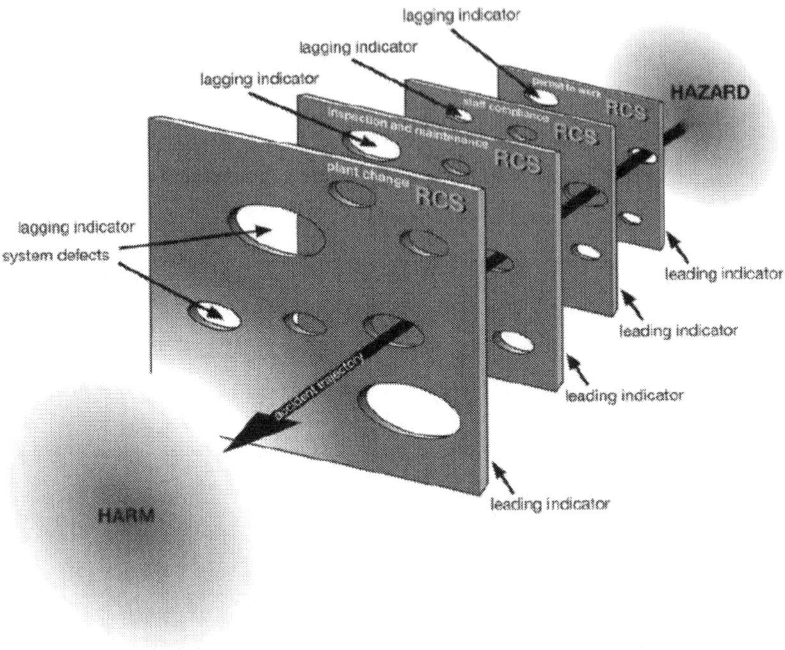

Figure 37: Swiss cheese model

The riskiest situations generally dictate a larger need for formality and rigorousness in the application of a MOC protocol. This may be in the form of a detailed written program that specifies exactly how changes are identified, reviewed and managed. Companies that have less risky situations can appropriately decide to manage change in a less rigorous manner, for example, through a general MOC policy that is implemented through informal practices by key, qualified personnel.

Facilities that present high demand for MOC may need more specificity in MOC procedures and a higher assignment of resources for personnel to carry out the defined functions and responsibilities. Facilities in which demand is lower can operate with more flexible MOC procedures. Facilities with a process safety management (PSM) culture, as shown in Figure 38, can choose to have more MOC procedures based on yield, allowing qualified employees to use common sense to manage change through an agile system.

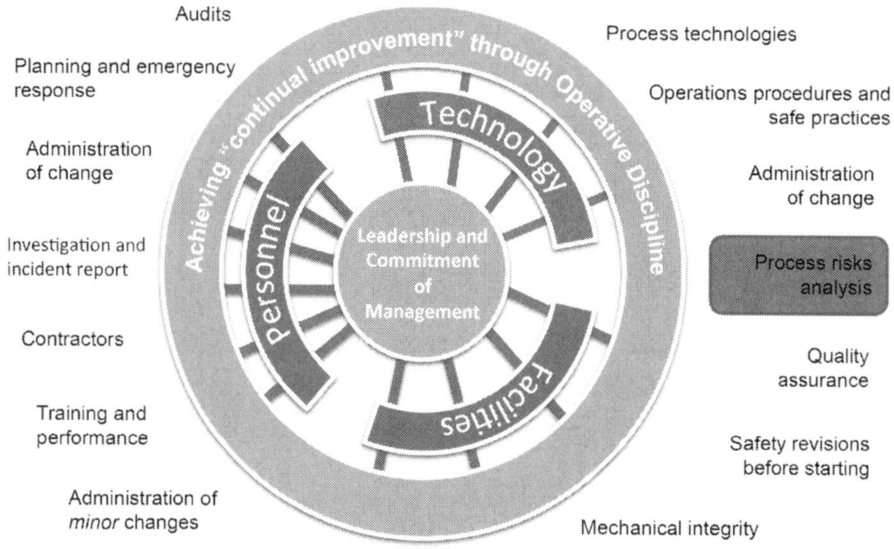

Figure 38: Process safety management (PSM), DuPont

Facilities with a culture of safety processes that evolve or are uncertain may require MOC procedures that are more prescriptive, where education is more frequent and more controls over functions and management systems are necessary to assure good MOC application.

Chef's Recommendations:

If the only thing that is constant in life is change, then the MOC process you manage must stay not only updated, but also must be efficacious.

In asset management, MOC is handled at two levels: in the implementation of the terms of asset management and the evaluation of performance and improvements. It is those points where an MOC effort in the asset management system is made at the level of processes, education, safety, etc.

Beware of changing an ingredient, evaluate the impact it could have!

THE ROLE OF THE ASSET MANAGER AND TYPES OF ORGANIZATIONS FOR ASSET MANAGEMENT

Direct Art and Technique of the Asset Manager

Peter F. Drucker, the all-time father of management, defines management as "the mission of the company which tries to motivate and organize human energies, with the objective of accomplishing that mission."

Therefore, the first task of an asset manager is to define the company's mission. And to define it correctly, you must orient yourself outwardly toward the market and the clients in the case of a commercial company or toward society if a public service organization. Asset management forms a part of the context of the organization, its stakeholders, and organizational plans and objectives under these ISO 55001 asset management requirements: *4.1 Knowledge of the organization and its context; 4.2 Knowledge of the needs and expectation of stakeholders; 5.1 Leadership and commitment; and 5.3 Roles, responsibilities and organizational authority.*

Defining the mission is a company task that demands the asset manager face management of change. No human institution is eternal, each changes during the course of time and according to the circumstances of its surroundings. The same happens with the mission; it must be redefined and updated periodically. The asset manager must have the capacity for analysis and deductive reasoning to know what is happening in the surroundings, which changes or new circumstances are problems and which are opportunities, what needs to be maintained and what must be changed.

On the basis of this knowledge, the asset manager has to make decisions, generate objectives and verify they have been met, and control the results. In this sense, the asset manager must be innovative and focused toward opportunities and results. In order to achieve this purpose, knowledge and the use of analytical tools are needed.

Being an asset manager is, above all, a profession and, as such, is not based on power or hierarchy, but rather individual responsibility. In this way, to be a manager and practice management, you don't need to occupy high-level positions, nor are subordinates needed. Assuming some sort of responsibility, having professional esteem and, most importantly, doing things consciously is sufficient.

Management is a liberal art whose purpose is human beings or human nature. People and their capacity to desire, imagine, think, create and feel are the motor of any society and its true riches. Without a doubt, techniques and technologies are important, but they are at the service of people, not the other way around.

The main object of management is to contribute to human development and progress, attempting to make the best of the resources that are at your disposal, especially the inexhaustible resources of human intelligence and avoiding any type of waste.

Principles and Functions of Modern Management

Referencing Peter Drucker once more, who leaves the key principles of his thoughts on modern management:

"Management is a PRACTICE, as is engineering, medicine, or law. And, in a practice, the basic work and fundamentals are ALWAYS elaborated and presented by PRACTITIONERS and not by academics. Only when a practice is sufficiently mature can academics make important contributions. And without PRACTICE, academics cannot produce contributions to MANAGEMENT."

Drucker's words indicate that understanding management isn't difficult, rather what is difficult is practicing it. The essential principles are simple and may even appear obvious to a lot of people. But those who make progress in a company almost always are the people who have a few basic principles clear and then, with dedication and effort, are capable of putting them into practice.

Asset Manager Tasks

1. Planning is the first task of the asset manager, who defines the company's mission and establishes the objectives that will be met in the future.

2. Every asset manager must dominate techniques to generate objectives and be able to establish a strategic asset management plan and asset management objectives. It's not about an academic luxury, but a necessity. Those who fail to direct the future have great possibilities of seeing themselves inundated by events.
3. The third task of the asset manager is to organize available resources according to the objectives of the plan. In a very special way, the asset manager knows how to organize his or her own time, one of the most valuable and scarce resources of any person's or organization's principal asset.
4. Above all, the asset manager must achieve a perfect union of human resources at his or her disposal and manage them properly. Companies with a high level of excellence are those that organize their resources by creating task forces, innovation groups, quality circles, or any other participatory system that assures that each and every person that makes up the company can contribute with all their capacities.
5. The asset manager must be an authentic leader, one who truly trusts the collaborators and practices in a real and decided fashion using delegation of authority techniques. Of course, a good leader always honors obligations and specific responsibilities, but knows that the key to success is in multiplying his or her productivity and capacity, achieving exceptional results with people's collaboration.
6. Control completes the management cycle, feeding back the system. The task of the asset manager is not to be on the lookout to see whether or not people are doing their jobs. Authentic control is an information process related to results that have been achieved by directing efforts toward the objective. What works is knowing which things have worked as predicted in the plan, which have worked worse than predicted and which have worked better.
7. The last task is continual improvement. The asset manager isn't limited to measuring deviations, rather using data provided by the control to make corrective decisions and continuously improve the work and results of the company.

These tasks are, in the end, the basic functions of modern management. When someone plans an activity, project, process, department and/or company and organizes the resources and means, acts directly or delegates and later controls the results, it can be said that person is an authentic asset manager.

But in each and every one of these phases, a decisive factor must always exist: motivation. If human energy is not mobilized, there will never be results, nor can any progress materialize.

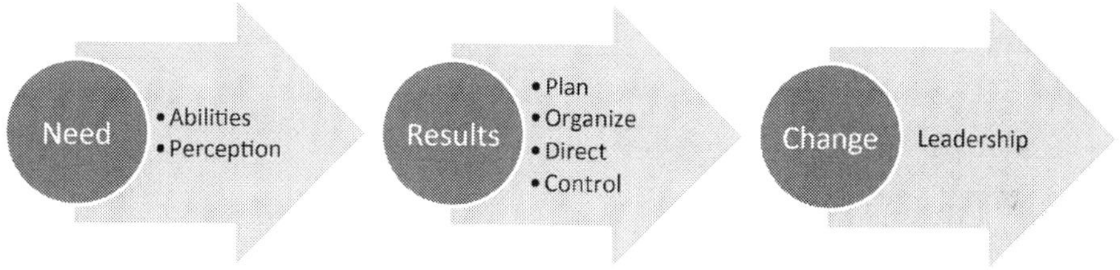

Figure 39: Asset manager's basic functions

Challenges Faced by the Asset Manager

In a society that can be described as dependent on technology, the asset manager must develop skills and perceptions to administer change at the same time speed, direction and reach. The technological factor, used not as a substitute for manual labor but as a novel application, leads to process management, which is another step toward the culture of change within organizations.

The asset manager of today finds obstacles, dangers and setups along the way that extend all the way through the path to success and self-realization. These include physical and mental exhaustion, marital or family problems, addictions and a shortened life span due to stress. These are only some of the dangers that asset managers must face.

On the other hand, the biggest reward and satisfaction for an asset manager is to construct a professional entity with the highest potential. The resources it will put under fire are those on the inside that will provide the capacity and intelligence necessary to administer in the most efficient way possible the asset manager's vision and those of the organization.

Direction of the Future

Implanting systems that can support your efforts to compete in the world is your immediate task. Making your current systems capable of creating better systems and these continue improving is an imperative you must accept. There is no choice if you wish to maintain control of your destiny.

Of course, there will be winners and losers. The transition will destroy very strongly held beliefs. There will be many who feel alienated by the acceleration of change or find no sense to the rapid destruction of structures of the conventional organization. The introduction of an open organization and the free flow will be chaotic to many. The concept of directing a time framed in the future instead of controlling activities of the present can become a meaningless activity, totally devoid of sense, to conventional directors. It's even probable the term "director" will disappear. The new technologies based on information technology will inhibit, in good measure, the capacity of directors from old generations to absorb and control changes that occur around them.

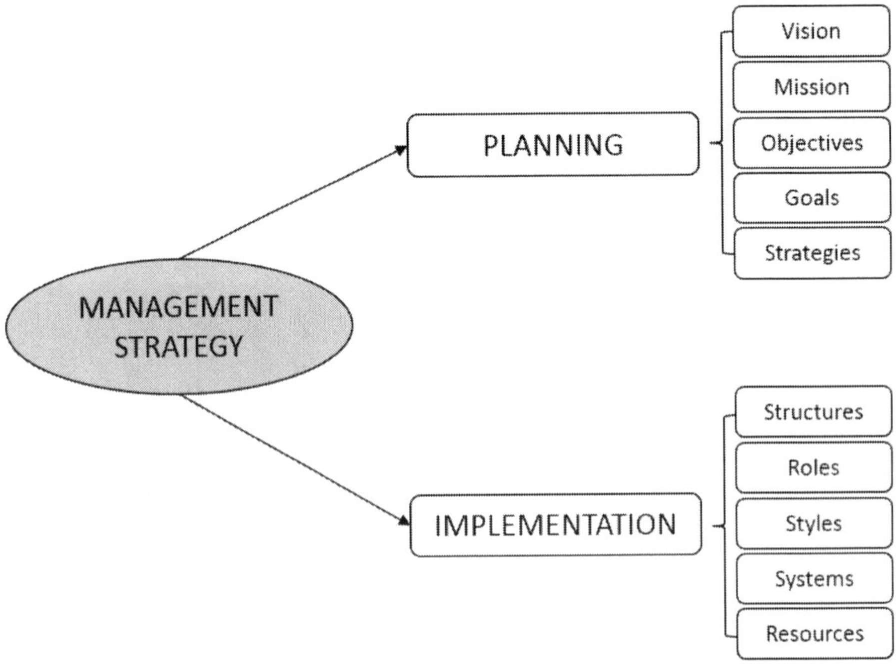

Figure 40: Management strategy

Global systems will disappear as information technologies start to assume the dominant role of conventional directors. Personnel that create added value will no longer need to base themselves on advice, specialization, or their superiors. In the new order, the idea of conventional subordination is a picturesque anachronism, in which a new type of barrier to communications will appear between the old and the new based on the possession of superior knowledge of technology and the capacity to exploit the potential of computers.

Multifunctionality of individuals will be found not so much in the expansion of intrinsic abilities, but via an individual's capacity to manipulate information systems that will solve problems without the intervention of the directive.

Real-time data introduced on computer webs will provide instantaneous information on organizational processes and allow the company, its suppliers and its clients to directly intervene in the system.

But in this context, you can't lose sight of ethics, which takes values into consideration and is the practice of deciding between the correct and the incorrect. A decision is ethical if it is considered acceptable behavior toward a recognized community or a standard group. If company objectives can be achieved only by breaking acceptable norms, then none of the decisions the company makes to achieve its goals will be ethical. As such, the objective turns into a dangerous practice because it will risk the company's future. With this way of proceeding, the vision and, therefore, the objectives, will be ethically corrupt and must be changed.

Ethical behavior means facing the consequences of decisions, particularly those referring to the influence on others. The new director should not do anything that means misuse of this intrinsic value. In the new order, a director must accept individual responsibility of the consequences of unethical decisions and corruption. Individual directors won't be able to hide behind a screen of corporate responsibility.

No director will be able to execute his or her function until demonstrating to the community that he or she has enough experience, both in the art of directing and in the knowledge of norms and ethical values. That way, continual improvement of ethical norms is possible, as well as essential to management practices, with many examples that prove it.

The Asset Manager as a Motivator of Change

Making changes in companies is a difficult and risky subject. Those who pretend to do it will find strong forces of resistance, given that changes typically generate costs in some internal company groups. If the process is not managed in a strategic way, it will surely fail. The key is in using adequate tools to execute effective leadership.

The essence of leadership requires people willing to put difficult problems on the table, people willing to swim against the current and established paradigms, people capable of generating tension, mobilizing tension, etc., but at the same time, people capable of containing pressure generated by change and conflict without decreasing adaptive work.

The leaders of tomorrow are those who are **open to change** and whose **self-esteem** is based on their **ability to adapt and grow.**

In 1943, the American psychologist Abraham Maslow formulated a theory on human motivations and called it Maslow's hierarchy of needs. It is represented by a pyramid that includes five steps or types of needs: physiological for survival; safety for protection; love and belonging; esteem for recognition; and self-actualization.

The need for self-realization is what moves human beings to find meaning in the things they do.

As Maslow pointed out, the last two pyramid steps are what move humans to find sense to their lives and develop all their potential in the service of their activity. This theory holds that as people begin to satisfy basic needs, they develop aspirations that are even more elevated and intrinsically related to the conquest of happiness.

At the beginning of the twenty-first century, a greater number of experts related evolution of conscience and human needs with changes that are slowly, but progressively, taking place in organizations. And companies are being impacted by this.

Right now, in order to attract, retain and motivate the best professionals (i.e., those who stand out for their enthusiasm, commitment and imagination), it's no longer enough to offer more money. Therefore, companies have no other choice but to focus on satisfying superior needs. Like Maslow described, these include belonging to a community, self-knowledge and demonstrating transcendental values.

This is the reason why companies are having to transform their work environments in such a way that they promote human relations of solidarity and spaces for personal and professional growth.

Materialistic Management Alone Is Not Enough

One of the obstacles regarding the drive to change is that leaders today were raised in yesterday's work environment, where the only focus was on material productivity, which did not take into account the human dimension of people. But, materialistic management is no longer enough. Either leaders change or the creative destruction process of the market will take care of changing the leaders. Dinosaurs of the material age have lost their niche and will become extinct, freeing resources for new business people of the mental and emotional age. In essence, the work world is immersed in a technological, social and emotional revolution.

Most veteran businesspeople tend to have the wrong idea about self-esteem. They look at self-esteem as knowing it all. On occasion, know-it-alls believe that what gives them value is the fact of having correct answers. Recognizing that yesterday's answers are not tomorrow's generates great reactivity and a sense of fear. These sensations are logical, given that if self-esteem is based on knowing it all, recognizing you don't know implies that the know it all must learn.

More humble and flexible businesspeople are those who show themselves open to change. Also known as learning leaders, there lies the essence of a true asset manager. An asset manager doesn't know it all, rather is in a process of learning. These businesspeople have a self-esteem that is based on their capacity to adapt and grow. They don't cling to yesterday's answers, rather they are much more interested in tomorrow. This change in conscience is what opens doors to later processes of innovation.

The key to self-esteem is based on the capacity to learn.

In moments of crisis and uncertainty, when strategies to achieve success show themselves to be volatile, when the known paths don't necessarily lead to the desired destination and your compass indicates you must not always head North, the importance of having learning leaders or asset managers emerges with clarity. It is important to understand, therefore, that leadership is a style of conduction that is committed to people's development.

"Leaders don't create followers, they create more leaders."

– Tom Peter

People who overcome the mental model of the know-it-all tend to have lived an awakening of conscience, provoked by the loss of a loved one, a personal project that fails, a professional failure, an illness and, in the end, a transformative experience that supposes suffering.

Who are you? What are your values? What is your mission? The true skeptic recognizes that they don't know and explore what they don't know.

Waking up means discovering who you are, what your most essential values are and what your true relationship with being is. In the past, these topics were exclusively for priests and psychoanalysts. However, in today's world, work is a perfectly adequate place to express your humanity.

However, many businesspeople show skepticism and cynicism in the face of this awakening. That's because they either poorly interpret the change or have taken a position before the experience and merely focus on destroying it without reaching an understanding of it. In the face of personal development, these types of people are convinced something doesn't work, denying themselves the opportunity to learn and grow. At the core, they are victims of their ignorance and their fear of recognizing it.

If workers only follow orders, they only generate accomplishment, not commitment.

Most bosses believe they pay a salary so workers follow orders. But this belief generates accomplishment and not commitment. Furthermore, following orders without thinking is very destructive for humans. People are not robots or machines, they are people with intelligence, emotions and souls. That's why stress and unfulfillment abounds. A true exchange means paying a salary to workers and giving them the opportunity to participate in a work society in which they can develop as individuals. In exchange for this, workers must make an effort to do their jobs, respectfully and cooperatively, and be interested in their own growth and development. In this way, they will generate added value for the company.

Creating the best work environment possible is aligned with the desire for profit.

Many businesspeople justify their reasoning by saying they barely have time to reflect on how to make healthy workplaces possible. But, it's not a matter of time, but priorities. The secret lies in how to use time in the best way possible. These types of businesspeople also tend to say that the desire for profit forces them to focus on the material and the tangible. This is also foolish because creating a better work environment is aligned with the desire for profit.

In order to make money, you needn't be authoritarian or merciless. Various research on this topic demonstrates that companies that make the most money are those **where people feel best.** People's satisfaction multiplies their ratios of yield and efficiency. So, it doesn't matter what businesspeople believe; if they want more benefits, they will have to learn to treat human beings as human beings and not as machines. Leading enthusiasm is much more productive than managing obedience.

Irrational leaders are those who don't realize when they live in times of crisis. With regards to this, Albert Einstein said: "Incompetence is the true crisis."

Einstein further stated: "Let's not pretend that things will change if we keep doing the same things. A crisis can be a real blessing to any person or nation. For all crises bring progress. Creativity is born from anguish, just like the day is born from the dark night. It is in crisis that inventiveness is born, as well as discoveries made and big strategies. He who overcomes crisis, overcomes himself, without getting overcome. He who blames his failure to a crisis neglects his own talent and is more interested in problems than in solutions. Incompetence is the true crisis. The greatest inconvenience of people and nations is the laziness with which they attempt to find the solutions to their problems. There's no challenge without a crisis. Without challenges, life becomes a routine, a slow agony. There's no merit without crisis. It's in the crisis where we can show the very best in us. Without a crisis, any wind becomes a tender touch. To speak about a crisis is to promote it. Not to speak about it is to exalt conformism. Let us work hard instead. Let us stop, once and for all, the menacing crisis that represents the tragedy of not being willing to overcome it."

The Project Management Office

A contemporary concept of the project management office (PMO) originated in the 1950s, when it was principally used in the armed forces or for critical projects that had special personnel to assure their accomplishment. Its purpose was to control specific projects and be closer to the client.

At the start of the 1960s, the concept of the PMO changed with regard to its functioning, users and expectations from the directive. While industry project developers (e.g., informatics, construction and defense) were the first to establish project offices for supervision and control, given they had mature projects and experience in the area of project management, productive chain industries (e.g., product manufacturers, companies from the primary and secondary sector) were focused on the optimization of their processes in the chain of value. Therefore, maturity in project management and the adoption of project offices were slowly adopted by these companies.

Although the majority of organizations are using project management to solve their problems, project promoters should adopt a broader application of project management disciplines and new modes to increase their effectiveness. Although agreement exists over what the acronym PMO means, there are variations on the definition of the function and role of a project manager's office, depending on the structure and function an organization intends to reach. In general terms, a PMO is an entity within the organization in charge of diverse responsibilities related to coordinated and centralized management of projects under its domain.

Some project management book authors have different perspectives on the exact nature of a PMO's functions. Among the PMO descriptions presented are:

"The guardian for the project management intellectual property."
– Kerzner

"A fundamental entity of an organization where a great variety of functions and structures are adopted, but where focus is on adding value to an organization and its clients in order to achieve the desired yield."
– Grey and Larson

Other authors define the PMO as a function that includes formalizing and integrating project management and coordinating multiple projects to help find the best performance with regard to quality, costs and time, which translate into an improvement in profitability of the organization.

The best project offices count on indisputable support from higher management, which demonstrates they are oriented toward the future.

On the other hand, some organizations have internally established their PMOs to reduce cost, but afterward they evolved into central entities for:

a. Managing individual, large projects;
b. Providing guidance, methodologies, tools and techniques;
c. Becoming centers of excellence that manage group projects.

As organizations search for more efficiency and higher yield from projects, they create project management offices that include the project management discipline. The PMO is becoming an important vehicle in organizations that provide project management services to support outputs meeting quality, cost and schedule, and contribute to performance via standardized practices and procedures.

Definition of an Asset Management Office

The asset management discipline has experienced significant changes, given the incorporation of standards like ISO 55001 (asset management) and EN16646 (maintenance within physical asset management). For a time, asset management projects were administered in a specific way; that is, each project was assigned to a manager that had previous technical experience in that subject. However, project failures and unmet goals led to the implementation of progressive changes in the form of directing these types of projects. This is how current asset management was born. It concerns itself with methods and techniques that can be applicable to projects of a different magnitude and complexity, with a focus that is strongly managerial, not merely technical. Project planning, follow-up and execution are proposed in a consistent and logical way, which came to be seen as a way of increasing the success of projects.

With the asset management discipline being recognized as a specific ability, the term asset management office (AM-O) became a way to describe an organizational unit responsible for processes of asset management projects.

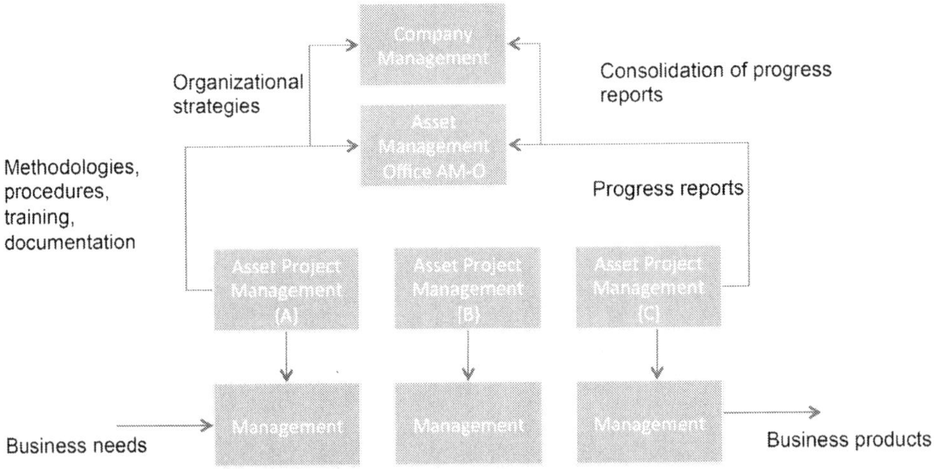

Figure 41: Conceptual scheme of an AM-O

In this way, the AM-O is the “home” for asset managers, where they find necessary support to administer projects on time, within costs and with the required quality and risk results via the use of methods and processes of planning, programming, follow-up and control, and closure. Apart from this, the AM-O is responsible for integrating the asset manager with the higher administration through a feedback system that allows for continual perfecting of the discipline in the organization.

Therefore, the AM-O can be defined as an entity within an organization consisting of personnel dedicated to providing a point of reference for the discipline of asset management.

An additional definition of an AM-O would be: an entity within an organization that has several assigned responsibilities for centralized and coordinated activities of those asset projects that fall under its jurisdiction.

AM-O Functions

The AM-O puts an emphasis on coordinated planning, prioritization and asset project execution linked to the asset management policy, the strategic asset management plan and the business objectives. As such, this office must be comprised of people who are trained in asset management and apply it to the use of good practices to drive continual progress in the management of assets and their lifecycle.

The function of an AM-O can vary based on what the organization needs it to be. It may be as simple as a few people preparing and maintaining assets and updating information, or made up of people who carry out planning, execution, report preparation, quality assurance and information collection on the performance of assets and their lifecycle.

An AM-O can be created to implement an asset management focus, develop standards, drawing plans and models for asset management, close gaps, etc. The responsibilities of an asset management office can extend from providing support functions for the direction of asset projects to the responsibility of directing projects directly.

So, AM-O functions can range from influence via consulting, to limited in recommending specific policies and procedures about the management of an asset's lifecycle from a technical or economic point of view, to a formal concession of authority on the part of the executive directive. In this case, an AM-O would delegate its authority as the director of an individual asset project. In this way, the asset manager would have administrative support from the AM-O through dedicated or shared personnel. The asset management team would include members who are dedicated to the management of assets, their lifecycles, or personnel who share other functions, but are directed by the AM-O.

In trying to keep asset management projects under control in terms of reach, costs, programming and quality, the AM-O plays an important role in managing a company's resources and providing assistance to obtain and assure the resources of diverse functional areas (i.e., enablers).

In addition, the AM-O is responsible for providing asset management policies, standards, procedures, skill building, software administration, information tools and asset management results.

Furthermore, it can participate in the selection, direction and movement of shared personnel dedicated to asset management projects (e.g., technological updates or new projects).

Given its mission for providing all necessary support for the management of assets and their lifecycle, and assuring projects are executed and aligned with asset management strategies, business policy and strategy, the AM-O also can provide services or internal consulting on all aspects of the organization in which project administration aptitudes are required.

Overall, the AM-O is a support unit of the company and the directors responsible for asset management.

Key AM-O Functions Within an Organization

Some of the most important functions of an AM-O within an organization are:

- Responsible for strategic planning of asset management, execution, follow-up, control and closure of projects;
- Responsible for identification, development and administration of policies, methodologies, standards and tools for managing the lifecycle of assets;
- Integrating information on projects and tools for management;
- Reporting the states of projects, in terms of CAPEX and OPEX to the company's directive and/or promoters;
- Responsible for developing asset management aptitudes;
- In charge of standardization and normalization of process planning, execution, follow-up, control and closure of asset improvement projects;
- Data preparation and dissemination of the lessons learned to avoid future failures in improvement projects and new projects that reflect the same errors;
- Recommend and implement management of change;
- Identify norms and good practices for the directive and asset management;
- Strategic planning of asset management, aligned with the policy and business plan;

- Coordination and/or development of educational programs for asset management;
- Transfer of knowledge through training and tutoring.

Additional functions of an AM-O focus on:

1. **Monitoring and controlling results of the asset lifecycle cost (LCC):** This is statistically the most important function. Managing the LCC includes tasks, such as providing asset status reports to higher management, implementing follow-up controls for asset performance, implementing an information system for monitoring and controlling assets, and developing an index table.
2. **Developing competencies and methodologies for asset management projects:** This includes the majority of functions traditionally associated with AM-O and has to do with the development of competencies for asset management. This includes: developing standard methodology, promoting asset management within the organization, developing personnel competencies through continual education, providing mentors for asset managers, and establishing a set of tools for asset management.
3. **Managing the asset portfolio:** Asset portfolio management has become an important aspect of asset management, as pointed out in ISO 55000, The Institute of Asset Management's "The Asset Management Anatomy," and the Asset Management Council's "Framework for Asset Management." These refer to the coordination of the interdependencies in a multi-active environment. Within these functions, the AM-O is responsible for coordination between enablers to identify, select and prioritize new asset projects, managing one or more asset portfolios and assigning resources.
4. **Managing the strategic asset management plan:** Providing consultation to higher directives regarding the business plan, participating in strategic planning and participating in the evaluation of CAPEX and OPEX proposals regarding optimization and replacement of assets, are activities that demonstrate the recent tendency for the AM-O to be more involved in the problems of strategic alignment and be a point of reference for higher directives.

5. **Organizational learning:** Although organizational learning is an important topic in management practices over the last few years, AM-Os should actively participate in organizational learning through functions, such as follow-up and control of asset projects, change management, internal audits of asset management aligned to ISO 55001, development of the asset lifecycle, implementation and management of the risk management database, and process safety management for the entire lifecycle.
6. **Additional functions:** These include specialized tasks for asset administrators, management of client interfaces, recruitment, and selecting and determining salaries for asset managers.

Organizational Models to be Implemented in Asset Management

The origin of asset management is linked to matrix type companies that possess a dual flow of authority, that is, vertical from the point of view of hierarchy and horizontal from the technical point of view. This type of structure is formed by the creation of teams with "enabler" members from several areas of the organization who carry out the asset management objectives, policies and strategic management of assets.

A matrix organization is an organizational focus that assigns specialists from different functional departments to work on one or more projects directed at asset management. The matrix structure creates a double chain of command that explicitly infringes on the classical principal of unity of command. The functional departmentalization is used to improve specialization. But, in parallel to functional departments, a series of managers exist who are responsible for specific products, projects, or programs within the organization.

Along the vertical dimension, the diverse asset management projects are added. Each asset management project is directed by a manager who integrates personnel from each of the functional departments of the company. The inclusion of a vertical dimension in traditional functional departments interlaces the elements of functional departmentalization and the product, thus the term, matrix.

Employees in the matrix have two bosses: the functional department boss and the asset manager. Asset managers have authority over functional members who are part of the team project. Authority is shared between the bosses under the direction of the asset manager.

To work in an efficacious manner, the two managers must communicate regularly and coordinate demands on employees.

Advantages:

- Several experts are on one team;
- Higher flexibility for the organization;
- Resources can be assigned to projects of higher importance from the strategic point of view;
- Helps mitigate conflicts between objectives generated by different functional areas of the organization;
- Members tend to be more motivated;
- Useful for training chains of command;
- Contributes to increasing the implication and commitment of team members.

Disadvantages:

- The dual flow of authority sometimes causes conflict;
- Can promote stress in team members by having to answer to two bosses.

An example of an organizational model to implement or optimize the asset management focus is provided at different levels: Strategic, see Figure 42, Tactical, see Figure 43 and Operative, see Figure 44.

At the strategic level, the organization of support and/or enablers is shown, as well as the definition of coordinators for each business area and the coordinator of initiatives related to the integrated management system (IMS).

At the tactic and operative levels in the different business units, those responsible for plants or central areas under each unit is shown and include most operative or technical levels (see Figure 44).

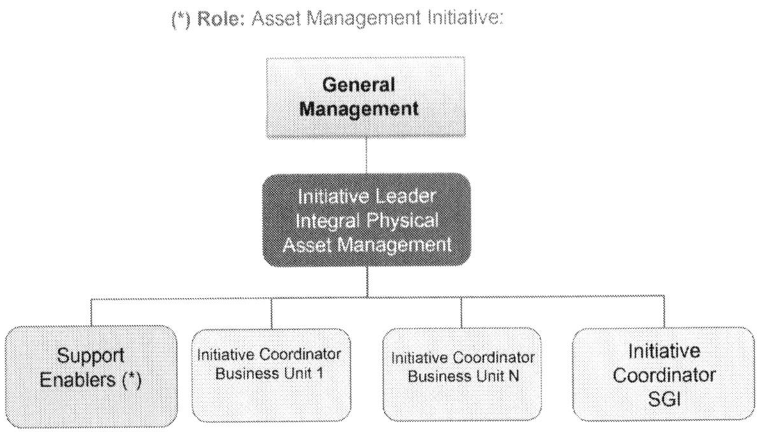

(*) Enabler organizations must assign a responsible person to supply documentation and required information for the implementation team (AM-O) and for the adaptation of asset management objectives and strategic asset management plan and policy to guarantee implementation guidelines with sustainability.

Note: Business unit for energy sector example: Distribution, generation, transmission etc. Example for a company in the oil and gas industry: Refining, production, perforation and transport. For the mining sector example: Mine and plant.

Figure 42: Organization strategic level (1)

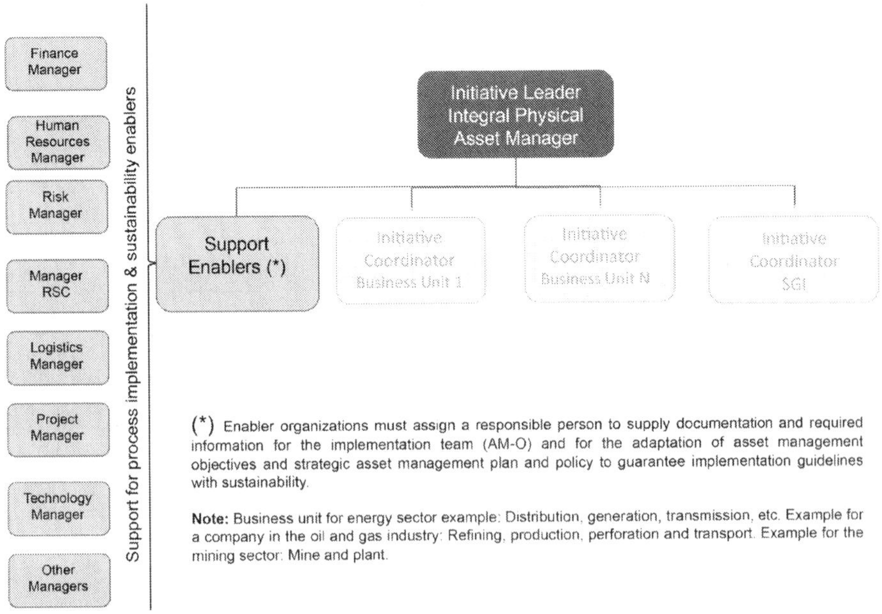

Figure 43: Organization strategic level (2)

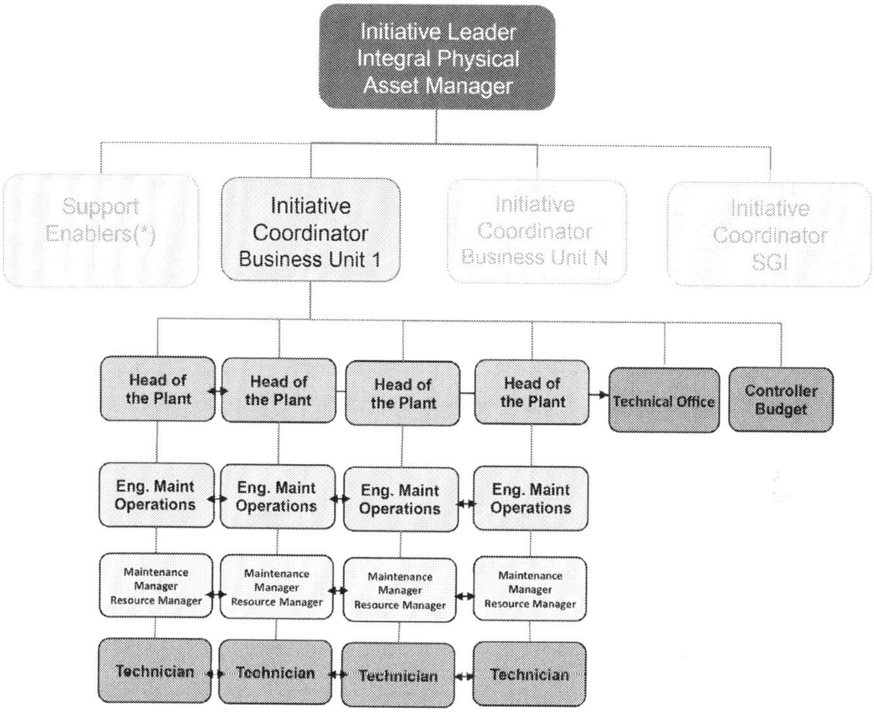

Figure 44: Organization tactical - operative level

Chef's Recommendations:

Chefs are nothing without a good team to help them coordinate in an adequate way the processes and areas of the kitchen. After the hustle and bustle and the tension it brings, one can say that the mission was accomplished when the last table is served and guests are satisfied.

In this sense, have you evaluated the type of organization you require and what competencies must be strengthened? This is one of the pillars of a successful implementation process, together with the development of a model.

ASSET MANAGEMENT POLICY, OBJECTIVES AND STRATEGIES

The Ingredients for Implementing an Asset Management Strategy

The number of organizations implementing physical asset management has increased since its birth decades ago. It's possible this increase is because technology requires the expert knowledge of a lot of people who have to work harmoniously to accomplish set objectives instead of the genius of one person working alone. Now comes the key question: What can the client do so the manager focuses on results? In reality, it's the client who directs. The client can demand, require, specify, as well as accept results.

How Is This Done?

The application of asset management models in industry has been possible thanks to a participatory culture, information transparency, communications, employee motivation, the delegation of authority and multifunctional groups. The decisions and results from the use of models, methodologies and standards, like ISO 55001, have reflected improvements in the contribution of companies to the clients' value chain.

Organizations of the information technology age are constructed on a new set of hypotheses and functionalities. These organizations work with integrated processes that interrelate traditional functions (e.g., operations, asset maintenance, purchases, finance, risks, environment, human resources, distribution, marketing and technology). They combine the benefits of the dominant specialization of the functional capacity with speed, efficiency and quality of integrated processes. Today's organization integrates the processes of provisioning with production in such a way that operations are activated according to client requests and not as a result of production plans that push products and services through the value chain. This improves costs, quality and response time.

The electrical, oil, gas, manufacturing and infrastructure industries, who now have to compete against the best companies in the world, don't escape this new way of doing things. New investments that demand new products and services may require having clients throughout the world providing adequate yield. That's why industry is combining efficiency and growing competitiveness of global operations with the marketing sensibility of local clients.

Companies compete in sectors of rapid technological innovation and must demonstrate themselves as leaders who anticipate future needs of clients, offer radically new services and use new technologies quickly in delivering efficient functioning processes and services.

This is why all employees must now contribute value, making use of what they know and the information they can provide. Investing in the knowledge of each employee and managing and exploiting said knowledge has become critical to the success of companies.

Aligning project objectives, budget, functions, business units and competency profiles with the strategic focus of the organization is the result of good practices found in applications created by the industry and supported by experience in organizations under a combination of tools and methods that can be applied according to need.

Implementation of the Strategy

Undoubtedly, the formulation of a different competitive strategy is vital to the survival of organizations. However, it's not enough. A strategy without effective implementation is merely a desire.

The strategic plan marks the vision of the desired future, while the real strategy is developed in practice through thousands of decisions made by the people of a company in their daily activity. So, reality makes evident the key aspect for a strategy to be implemented in an effective way in an organization with the commitment of all its members.

It is here where the asset management system (ISO 55001) as a strategic management plan helps in the implementation of the strategy, as shown in Figure 45.

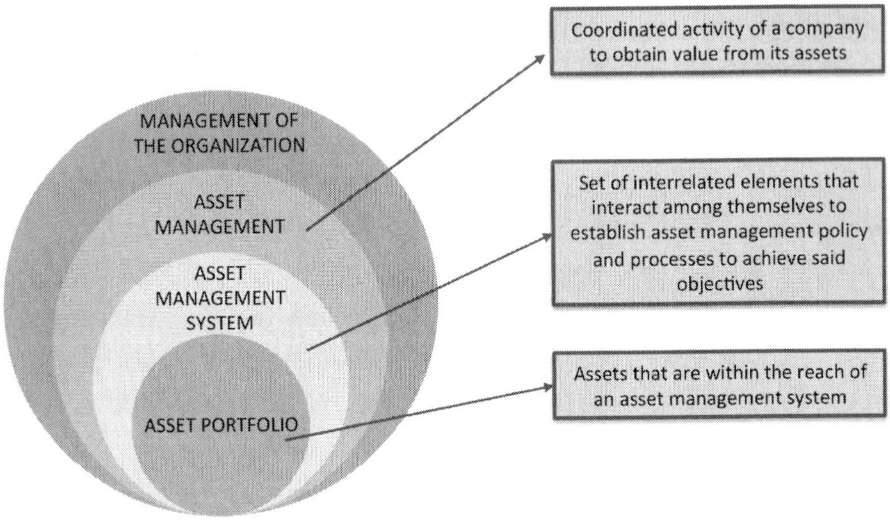

Figure 45: Relationship among key terms *(ISO55000, 2014)*

The Barriers to Implementation

Various studies reveal four major implementation difficulties in a maintenance, operations and projects organization.

1. **The strategy cannot be put into practice.** The strategic vision hasn't been translated into an operational strategy that can be put into action, communicated and understood throughout the organization. According to studies, only forty percent of intermediate managers and five percent of employees truly understand the strategy and the way of contributing to its development (see Figure 46).
2. **Management of people isn't aligned with the strategy.** Personnel objectives and incentives linked to results in the short term aren't necessarily aligned with the long-term objectives that define the strategy. Only twenty-five percent of executives have incentives linked to strategic objectives.

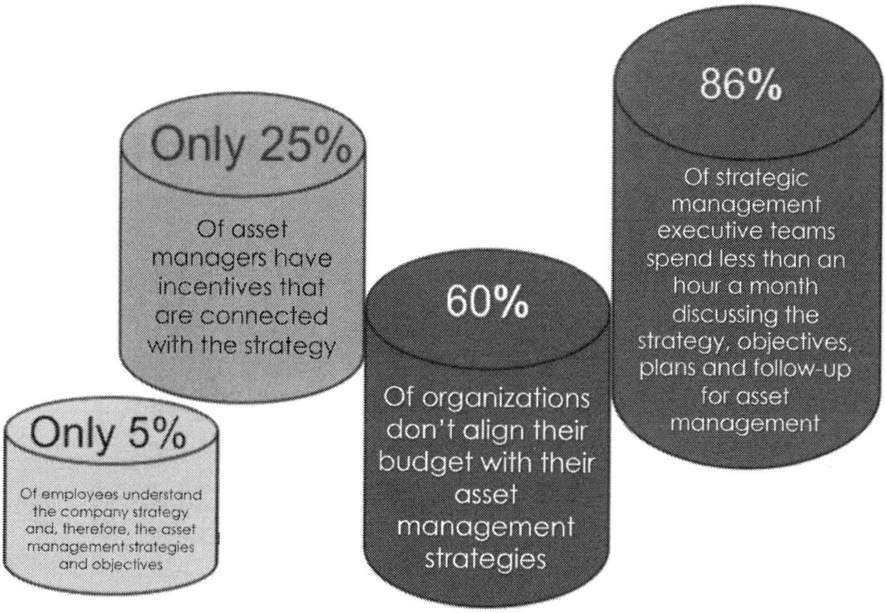

Figure 46: Why do strategies fail? *(Amendola. L., 2011)*

3. **The organization, process and budgets are not aligned with the strategy.** The assignment of resources (i.e., budgets), the models of the organizational structure and the processes depend more on financial criteria in the short term than on the strategic objectives defined. Sixty percent of companies do not align their budgets with the strategy.
4. **Information mechanisms are tactical, not strategic.** Information mechanisms focus on measuring and reporting, promoting control and not learning, and shared management of knowledge. Eighty-six percent of directive teams dedicate less than an hour a month to tackling strategic topics and fifty percent never do it at all.

Key Factors for Implementing an Asset Management Strategy

Success factors for good design and implementation are: leadership on the part of higher directives of asset management; good communications and participation; adequate constitution and effort by the team; and considering barriers to change and people's responsibilities. The integrative and global focus provided by norms and standards makes implementation difficult, but not impossible. It's about being clear on the aspects that can smooth the ground for implementation.

Those ingredients are:

A simple plan: The objective of a strategic plan isn't to add bureaucracy or complications, rather to simplify project management by focusing on what is important. The key word is prioritization. It's about ordering information, projects and resources in an efficient way for the organization.

Common language: The name given to the plan, perspectives and the different elements that compose it are of least importance. What is important is that people use them to arrive at a consensus. There needs to be a common language for organizing physical assets, whether the plan is called, for example, balanced scorecard or integral management table, the name makes no difference.

Understanding the plan: No two companies are alike and no two implementations are alike, either. Companies must adapt plans to suit their own needs. In principle, all elements must play a part and it's important they are understood. Deviations from the strategic plan can be justified, in some cases, but the justification must never be ignorance. Therefore, it's important that the strategic plan for asset management be properly understood at the start of a physical asset management implementation project.

Leadership: Transmitting the relevance of the project to the organization is necessary and it must be led and supported at the highest level of the company. This leadership must be continuous and not only in the initial stage of the asset management project.

Communications: In order for the strategic plan to be accepted, it must be understood and internalized by the people working in the organization. Therefore, a good communication process, both vertical and transverse, is necessary.

Participation: The participation of certain people who can provide value also helps to internalize the strategic asset management plan. Participation also enriches the design of the different elements that compose it.

Asset management project team: It is vital to assign a team or facilitators to manage implementation. Their task is to facilitate knowledge, provide methodology and follow-up on the project.

Key Elements and ISO 55001 Requirements

The specific asset management standard, ISO 55001, establishes a relationship between the terms asset portfolio, asset management system, asset management and management of the organization.

The standard is composed of ten key elements and twenty-three requirements, which cover asset management reach in an organization. These key elements and requirements provide the context and global direction of activities in the organization, including asset management activities (see Figure 47).

General Description of the Asset Management System

Generalities

Higher management, employees and interest groups in an organization should implement planning, control activities, such as policies, processes and follow-up actions, and follow-up activities to make the most of opportunities and reduce risks to an acceptable level.

The management of assets implies an equilibrium in the costs, risks and yield of assets in order to achieve the objectives of the organization. However, it's possible equilibrium will need to be considered in different time lapses.

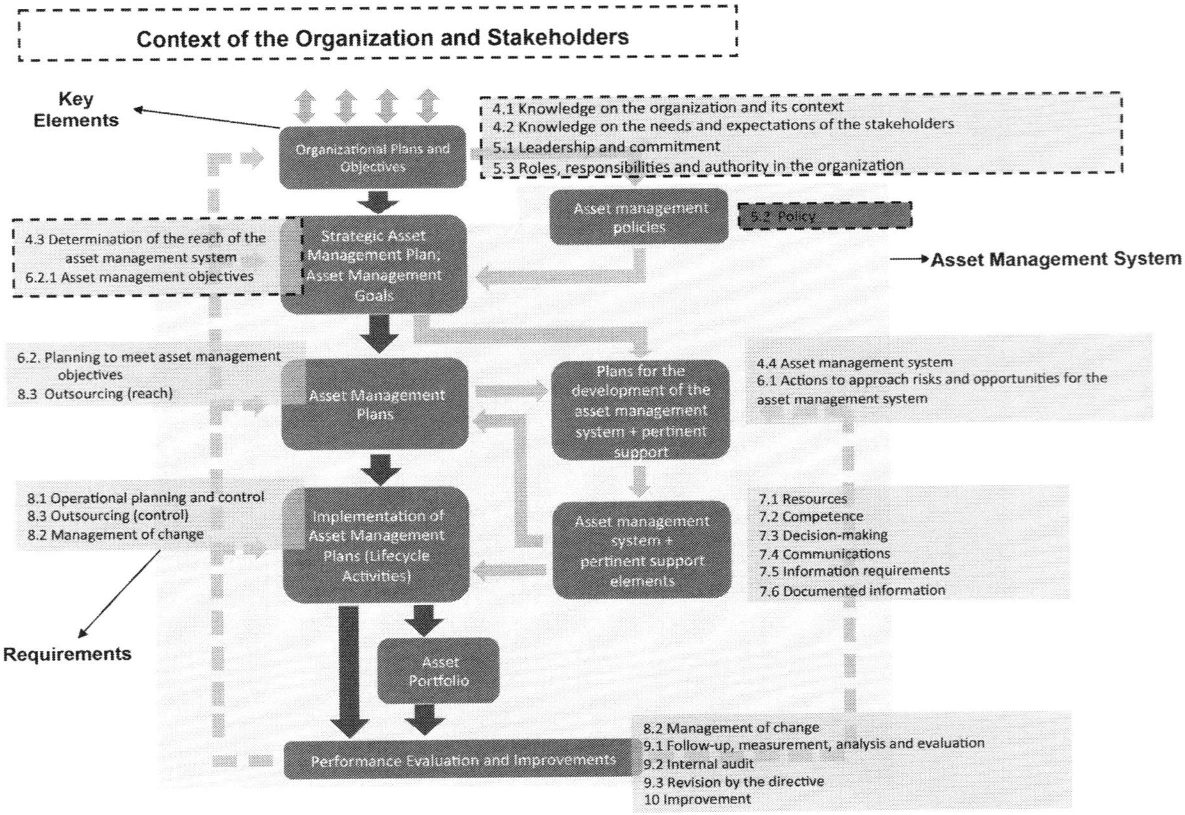

Figure 47: Key elements and requirements *(ISO55000, 2014)*

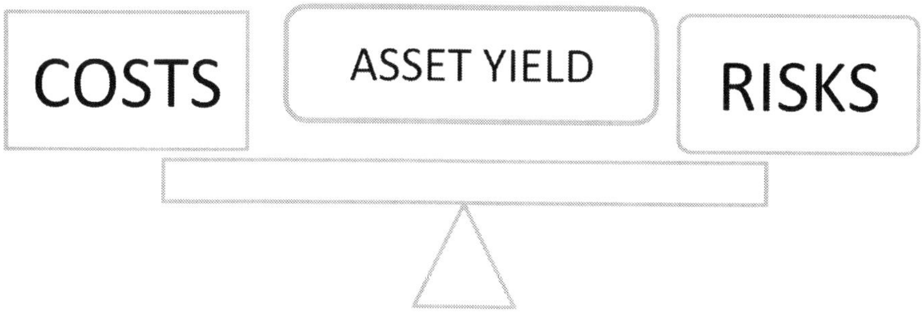

Figure 48: Equilibrium factors

Fundamentals

Asset management is based on a set of fundamentals. These are:

Value – Assets exist to provide value to the organization and its interest groups. Asset management is not focused on the asset itself, but on the value the asset can provide an organization. This value, which can be tangible or intangible, financial or non-financial, is determined by the organization and its interest groups according to the objectives of the organization (Figure 49).

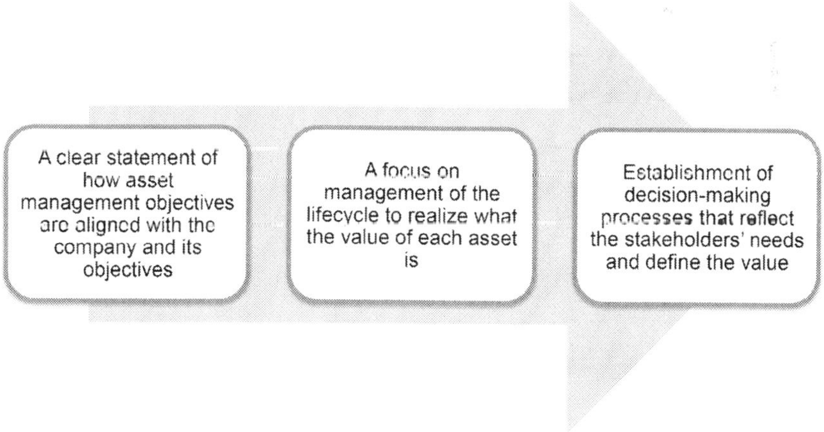

Figure 49: Values in the organization

Leadership – Leadership and workplace culture determine value generation in an organization. Leadership and commitment at all levels of management are essential for establishing asset management in an organization with success, functions and improvement (Figure 50).

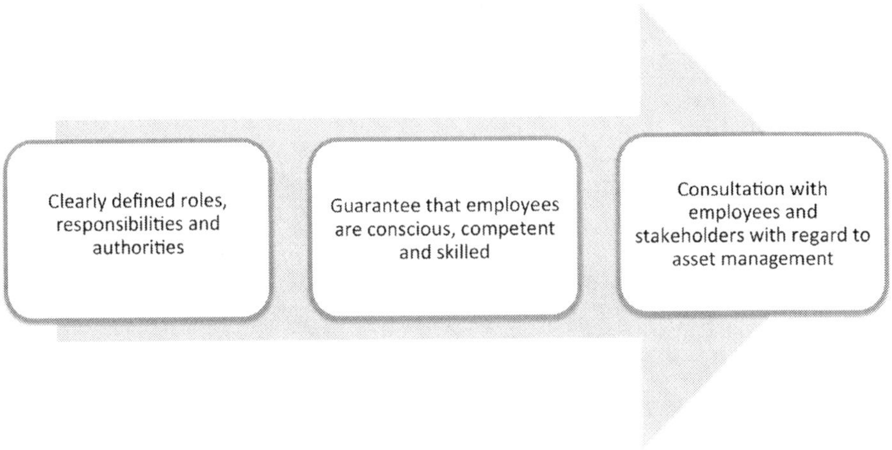

Figure 50: Roles and leadership in the organization

Assurance – Asset management gives assurance that assets will meet the required purpose. The need for guarantee comes from the need to efficaciously govern an organization. This assurance is applied to assets, asset management and the asset management system (Figure 51).

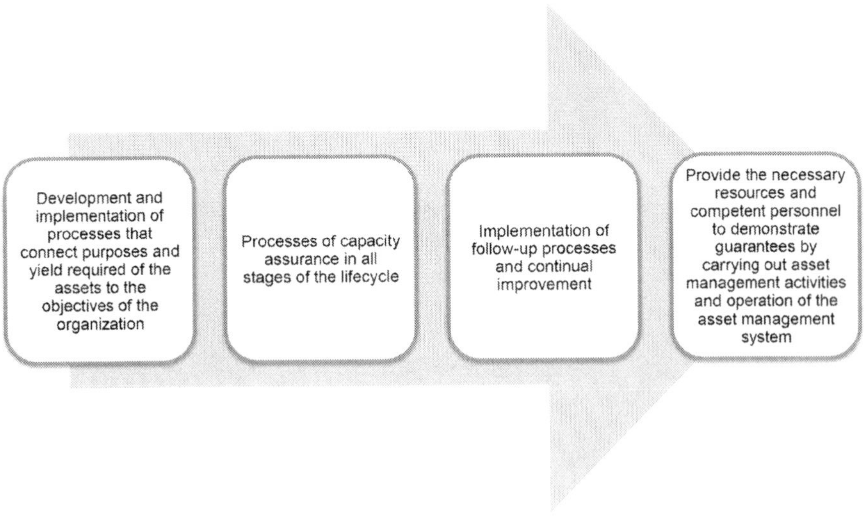

Figure 51: Assurance of asset function

Alignment - Asset management translates organizational objectives into technical and financial decisions, plans and activities (Figure 52).

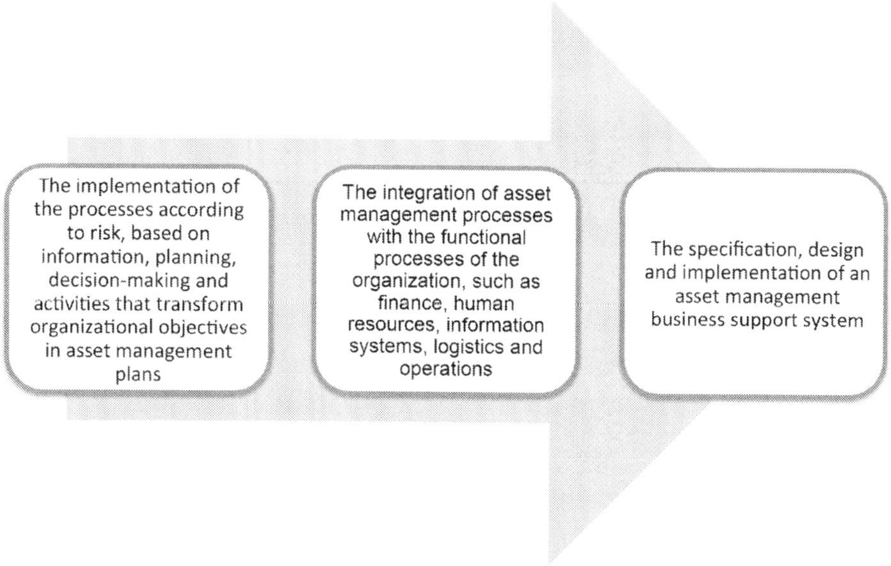

Figure 52: Alignment in the organization

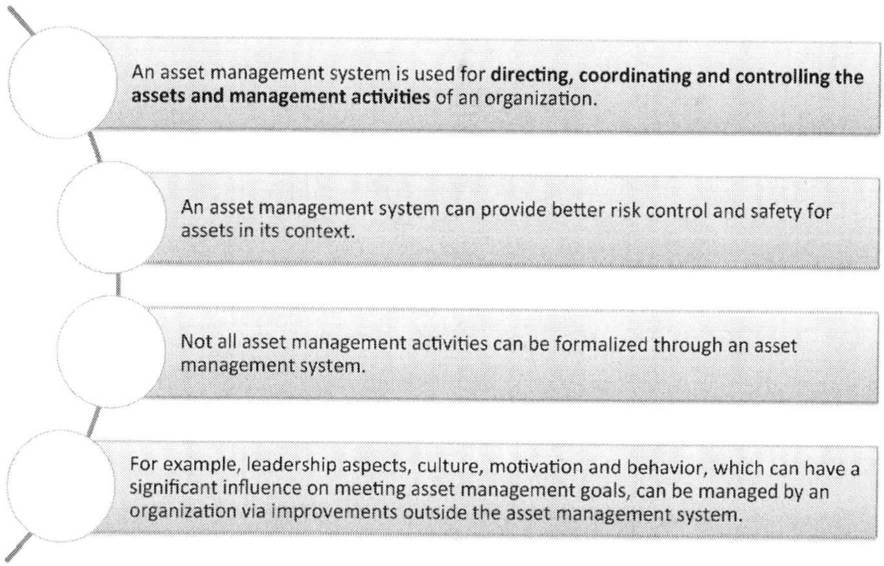

Figure 53: Relationship among key terms

What Is a Policy?

Policies are general statements or ways of understanding that guide thought and action in decision-making for all members of an organization.

Company policy defines how things in the organization should be done. For example, "In this company, things are done following this procedure." It doesn't matter whether the company is in the same sector or subsector, its policies can be diverse.

One of the purposes of policies is to give a unified structure to strategic plans, avoiding analysis and repetitive processes and, in the same way, easing delegation and control. In a big company, where quality makes it necessary to standardize production and processes, it's essential to count on guidelines that guide the action of each operator without having to always consult with supervisors to know whether expected results are being obtained. In this sense, policies provide a special value for any type of company, both big and small.

It's much easier to carry out the phases of process control and verification of results for self-regulation and its improvement when policies are followed.

Asset Management Policy

An asset management policy is a brief statement that establishes the principles for how the company will apply asset management to achieve organizational objectives. High directives should authorize the asset management policy, therefore demonstrating the company's commitment to asset management.

The expectations and commitments stated in the policy should cover decisions, activities and behaviors related to asset management. Additionally, it should be aligned with and demonstrate support for organizational objectives. For example, if an organizational objective is to reduce capital investment, a statement in the asset management policy would focus on risks for capital investments.

Here are examples of some principles or commitments of asset management policies:

- Guidelines for asset management activities, for example, the objectives for providing services serve as a guide for practices and decisions of asset management;
- Adherence to applicable laws, legislation and regulations;
- The resources to meet asset management objectives and the structure or function of the organization to meet organizational objectives; for example, planning and asset management should be integrated with planning, budgeting and reporting processes of the corporation or business;
- Decision-making criteria to be used, for example, asset management decisions should be based on evaluating options that consider costs of the lifecycle and benefits and risks of the asset;
- Reports on asset performance and asset management;
- Long-term objectives, sustainable results and requirements of stakeholders;
- Continual improvement of the asset management system.

A policy needn't be compiled in a separate document; it can be contained in other policies or high-level organizational documents. For example, it can be included in the strategic asset management plan. What's important is that it is communicated to the organization. If this can be demonstrated, a separate document is not required to make reference to the asset management policy.

Established processes should exist for reviewing and updating the asset management policy and to assure necessary actions will be taken to update the policy should external or internal context change.

Here is an example of an asset management policy for the fictional company, Energy4U:

With the purpose of meeting strategic objectives, Energy4U is committed to achieving world-class performance of its assets through operational excellence.

To this end: Energy4U commits to safe, sustainable and environmentally responsible functioning of all its assets. Also, Energy4U has the commitment to maintain a continual improvement process to provide excellent asset yield that meets or exceeds commercial and technical objectives. And, lastly, Energy4U commits to guaranteeing reliability and integrity of assets throughout their lifecycle at optimum cost.

In order to achieve this, Energy4U will do the following: Assure that health, safety and environmental objectives are key to the entire organization and operations and maintenance (O&M) service providers, business strategies, plans and goals. Assuring the existence of an organizational structure with a clear responsibility for execution and review of all aspects of asset management also must be carried out.

Energy4U will keep a register of the condition and the risks of critical assets and a long-term plans for assets. This will be complemented with benchmarks, establishing and monitoring world-class performance goals according to norms and meeting ISO 55001's asset management framework.

Additionally, it must assure O&M service providers work under world-class standards and an O&M framework that is appropriate and has defined procedures that are implemented.

Energy4U will manage world-class planning, execution of plant stops and optimal capital investment. For this, it will be necessary to invest capital as necessary to maintain and improve asset yield and their lifecycle. All of this will be done with the aim of driving continual improvement of costs and income through the optimization of costs and controlled mechanisms.

Through the provision of O&M services, Energy4U will assure aspects, such as:

Plants must obtain and maintain required standards of excellence associated with health, quality, safety and the environment.

The establishment of annual maintenance plans for all assets should be assured. At the same time, verify the comprehensive use of a maintenance management system to assure that each asset has relevant, up-to-date information, as well as the registration and control of correctives, preventives and predictives, and the historical record of the plant.

All O&M activities are to be carried out by fully qualified and competent personnel. To ensure that plants are operated and maintained with the best practices of the industry and O&M providers maintain a commitment to continual improvement, activities must be demonstrated through periodic and detailed presentations of yield reports.

Strategic Asset Management Plan

The strategic asset management plan (SAMP) is a document derived from the strategic business plan. The SAMP shows the strategies and specific actions for implementing an optimal management focus for physical assets in projects the company undertakes to meet the objectives of the organization.

By translating the strategic plan of the organization into specific strategies for physical assets, the SAMP helps guide activities and decision-making in an organization. The initiatives defined in the plan should be reviewed regularly to guarantee applicability in a changing environment and to incorporate feedback for the economic context, country and community.

Not to be confused with the company's asset management model, the SAMP should not include asset management policies, practices and procedures, as this information can be found in detail in specific documents related to those aspects, such as the asset management policy and guidelines for implementing the asset management model. Likewise, more detailed information on individual assets, other policies, operational and legal matters, and maintenance strategies can be found in support documents inside the management system and in the plans the organization currently has.

Based on the results of context reviews, stakeholders' recommendations and results from the GAP analysis and the 3Ps and SAM tools, the asset management organization should define the limits of the asset management system and establish its reach in order to develop the strategic asset management plan.

The limits and applicability of the asset management system should be stated as part of the reach of the strategic asset management plan. It should be communicated to all pertinent stakeholders, both internal and external. The details of the plan will be influenced by the size of the organization and the scale and complexity of the asset portfolio covered by the asset management system. What is considered inside and outside the reach should be clearly shown.

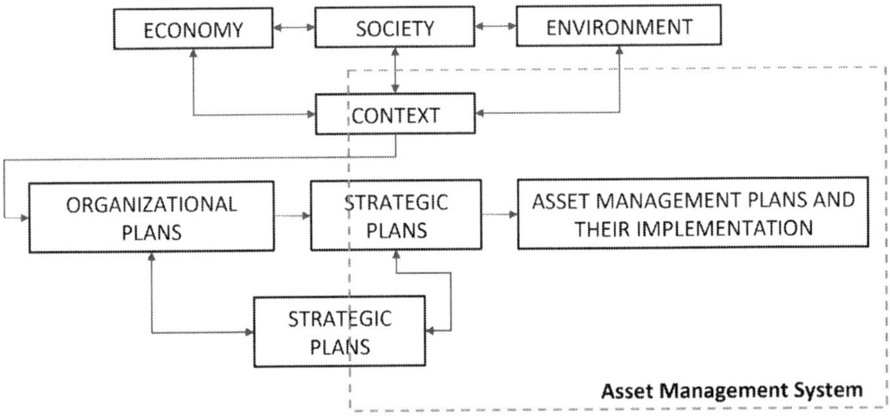

Figure 54: Asset management system integration *(Amendola, L., 2015)*

The reach of the strategic asset management plan should consider:

- Assets, asset portfolios and their limits and interdependencies;
- Other organizations involved in meeting the asset management system's requirements (including ISO 55001 requisites), for example, through outsourcing of asset management activities or activities related with stages of the lifecycle;
- Organizational aspects, for example, the parts and functions of the organizations involved;
- The period of responsibility of the organization if asset management is outsourced for a certain period of time, including residual responsibilities beyond the operation and use of the asset, for example, how long the organization continues to be responsible for a chemical plant that maintains responsibility for soil contamination;

- The interaction with all parts of the management system of the organization, for example, management of quality or the environment, that can require the definition of limits, functions and responsibility of each part of the management system.

What organizations should consider when designing a strategic asset management plan:

- Review risks of asset failures, including potential impacts;
- Asset management activities to achieve the asset management objectives in an individual and combined way;
- The importance of assets with regard to the proposed results, objectives and requisites of products or services;
- The applicability of asset management objectives during the asset management planning process.

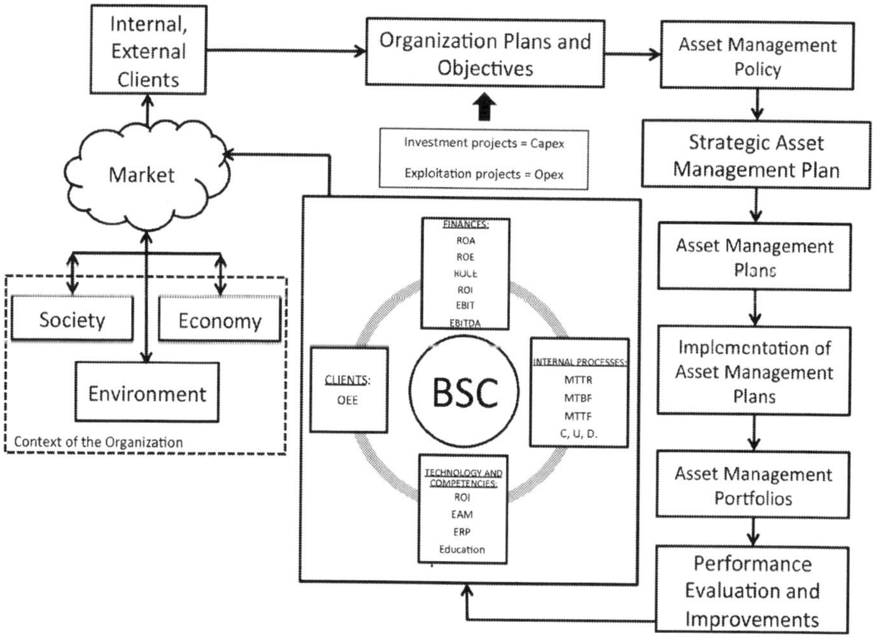

Figure 55: Sustainability model aligned with asset management *(Amendola, L., 2015)*

The strategic asset management plan approaches matters that typically include, among others:

For asset management:

- Total cost of the property
- Net Present Value (NPV)
- Return on invested capital (ROIC)
- Performance relative to that planned
- Certification of the asset management system or evaluation of the maturity of asset management (e.g., benchmarking, market comparison and SAM diagnosis)
- Client satisfaction scoring
- Results of public opinion and reputation polls
- Environmental impact, for example, costs related with carbon emissions
- Service level

For asset portfolios:

- Return on investment, ROIC, or return on assets (ROA)

For asset systems:

- Availability of the asset system, mean time to repair (MTTR), mean time between failures (MTBF), mean time to fail (MTTF)
- Asset management system performance, for example, time working, efficiency, overall equipment effectiveness (OEE)
- Unit cost of the product or service

For assets:

- Reliability and maintainability (MTTR, MTBF, MTTF)
- Condition, performance, or asset health scoring; asset lifecycle cost (LCC)
- Energetic performance of the asset.

Key Elements of the Strategic Asset Management Plan

Figure 56 shows the key elements associated with strategic planning for physical assets. The strategic business plan and objectives cover the key elements. As illustrated, physical asset management is fed by the responses to these questions:

- Where are we going?
- What are we going to do in five years (based on the previous Energy4U strategic plan example)?
- What will we do each year (i.e., annual operative plan).

On the other hand, Figure 56 shows the pillars of physical asset management as: asset management policy, asset management strategy, asset management plans (i.e., required resources) and the assurance of funds required to carry out the asset management plans.

Essentially, the general objectives of SAMP are:

- Establish high priority strategies and actions in association with the development of actions necessary for the optimization of physical asset management projects in which the company operates;
- Define the required organization and roles for the development of strategies to achieve the focus of optimal physical asset management;
- Facilitate the transformation of strategic objectives of the company into strategic objectives of asset management and communicate, execute and measure them;
- A fundamental management tool for maximizing long-term benefits through socially responsible guidance.

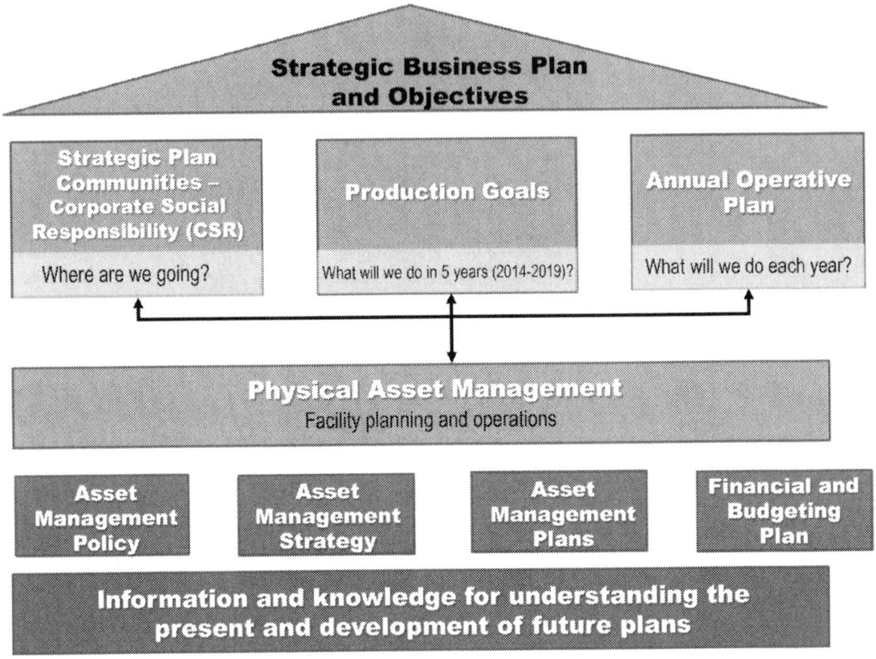

Figure 56: Key elements of asset management strategic planning

(Amendola, L., Depool, T., 2012)

The SAMP is oriented toward a specific form of developing concrete actions on: information quality and knowledge on assets; efficacy of communication of data and information; orientation toward a proactive focus; and optimization of operative costs and answering new growth challenges from the proposed percentage. All this is performed under a scheme of optimal equilibrium between costs, personnel safety, process safety, environmental respect, personnel development, reliable response to the market and contributing to economic and social development.

Strategic Framework for Physical Asset Management

The strategic framework for physical asset management is the reference through which the objectives of asset management will be met. In this sense, the framework is comprised of the:

- Strategic plan and strategic objectives;
- Guidelines for visible practices associated with implementing the asset management model;
- Policies and strategies for asset management at the strategic level with regard to:

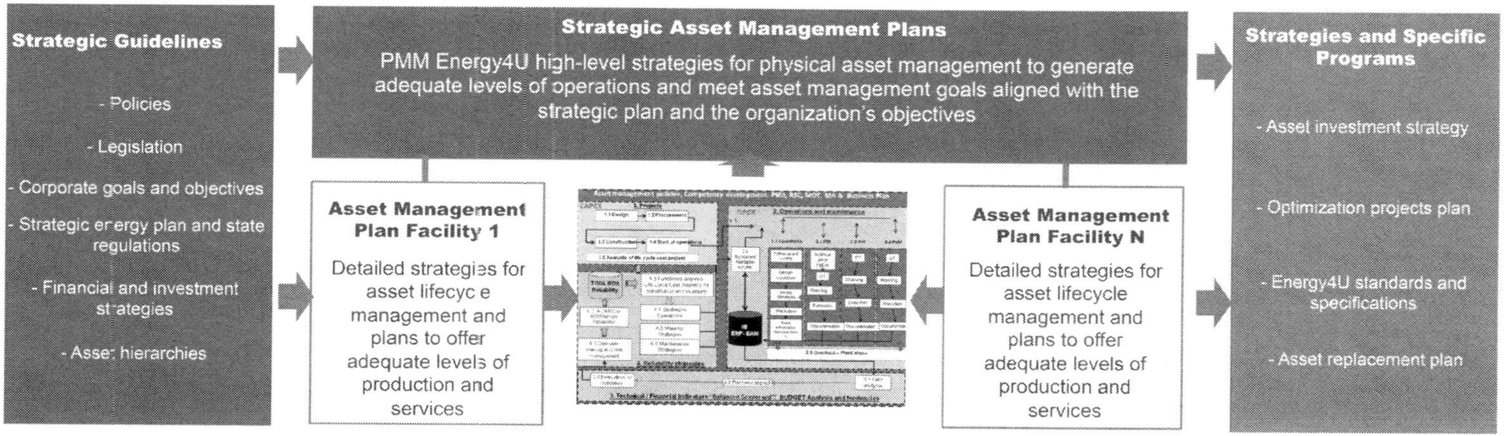

Figure 57: Strategic asset management plan

- Current and future demand;
- Sustainability, operative integrity and process safety management (PSM);
- Optimized management of physical asset lifecycle;
- Information system for physical asset management;
- Continual improvement and a focus associated with the optimization of costs;
- Management of goods and service providers related to physical assets;
- Management of knowledge and development of compe tencies aligned with asset management;
- Management policies and strategies;
- Financial consequences of the actions taken;
- Management of risk and management of change (MOC);
- Social, economic and legal matters;
- Development of competencies in physical asset management;
- Detailed and documented plans for strategies specific to assets;
- Evidence and evaluation of continual improvement.

Figure 57 outlines the structure of the framework for the strategic management of assets. It should be noted that part of the strategic guidelines at the level of the specific definition for the asset management plan stems from the high-level strategic plan. The management of assets for the projects or plans in which they currently operate (the Energy4U example) is directed by the asset management model that has been selected by the company (the integral physical asset management model of PMM example).

Chef's Recommendations:

As a key to success, it is indispensable for an organization to consider evaluating which of the ingredients it needs to develop an adequate plan for implementing its asset management system.

The evaluation and selection of ingredients are as vital as the decorations on the table and plate presentation.

But, be wary of recipes. If you are only guided by recipes and don't know what you are cooking, it's possible you won't obtain the expected result. For example, if you only know how to follow a recipe, you are unable to see an imprecision in it, such as a recipe from Germany that doesn't consider the temperature or altitude of where you are. This variable can cause the cooking times to be longer.

MAIN DISH (building sustainability)*

Chicken, Rabbit and Greens Paella (Serves 4)

Preparation

1. Pour oil in the center of the paella pan and level it around the pan. Turn heat to medium and heat the oil.
2. When the oil starts to smoke, lightly salt the chicken and rabbit and add them to the pan. When golden, turn the meats carefully. (It's very important that all the meat is properly golden, the success of the paella depends a lot on this step and preparation.)
3. Add the beans and snails and cook for a few minutes.
4. Add the tomato and chopped garlic. Sauté them for a few minutes, lower the heat and add the pepper. (It's important that the heat be low at the time of adding the pepper, as you can run the risk of burning it and the paella will taste bitter.) Let cook for a minute and add the water almost to the top.
5. Let it cook for around 20 minutes, adding more water and salt if necessary.
6. After 20 minutes, add the rice. (You must make sure the paella broth reaches halfway to the rivets of the handles when adding the rice.)
7. Add the saffron to the rice, as desired (in strands, toasted, ground, diluted....). Mix the rice uniformly and make sure no grains of rice end up on top of the meat or beans without being submerged in the broth. Cook at very high heat for 8 minutes or until the half cooked rice starts to poke out. Cook 10 minutes on low heat.
8. Let rest for a few minutes and enjoy!

Ingredients (4 persons)

- ½ chicken, chopped
- ½ rabbit, chopped
- 400 gr rice
- 150 gr green beans
- 150 gr lima beans
- 1 tomato, grated
- 1 garlic clove, chopped
- 1 tablespoon sweet pepper
- Salt
- 100 ml extra virgin olive oil
- 16 snails
- 6 strands of saffron
- Water

*Authentic Valencian paella recipe, Acknowledgments: Mornell Restaurant and www.mornell.es

Chef's Comments:

The star dish; the price of Valencian cooking "structured" in the form of earth ingredients, a lot of temptation and patience.

Are you up for it?

Reflection: Cooking and Asset Management

After the starters, that is, after preparing the stomach, now you are ready to taste more ingredients and receive the main dish.

It's important to prepare the stomach well in order to prevent bad digestion.

Making the analogy to asset management means preparing the foundation well, having knowledge about why proposed actions are being implemented, where it will all lead the organization and what the expected results are.

Dessert

KPI ASSET MANAGEMENT INDICATORS

Budgeting for Asset Management

How much expenditure should there be for asset management? This question is easy to ask, less easy to answer and even more complicated to understand. Obviously, it is bad business to spend too much, as is spending too little, in asset management.

As a rule of thumb, most like to use an estimation method done on the basis of a practical rule. It's not based on science or an exact measure and it is often confused with benchmarking. However, comparative evaluation implies a more exact measure and knowledge of the underlying cause and effect. In order to get to be the best, you need to compare yourself and learn from that comparison.

The most common question executives, technicians, engineers in the industry and my students ask me is:

"What are the appropriate points of reference for asset management costs?"

You can all use tools and available information to calculate your costs for the following year and its tendencies based on market movements and the economy. But, the most important question for a business on its expenditures in physical asset management isn't where you are going to be in the present, but rather where you will be in the future. And for this, one must answer the following question:

What is optimal for my business?

The following explanation details how to carry out an evaluation on the basis of reference data, like key performance indicators (KPIs), and provides a guiding path to accomplish the goal.

The Path to Take: a sustainable focus for the optimization of budgeting for asset management.

So, how do you proceed when demands for optimization of costs are higher every time?

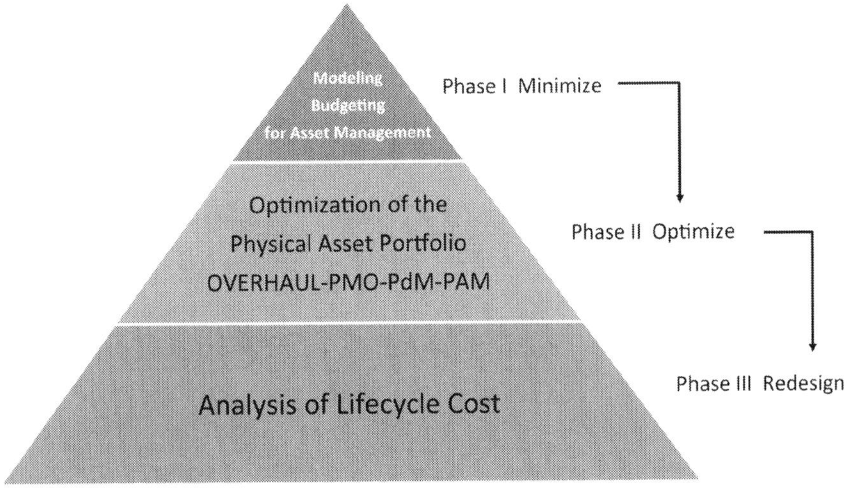

Figure 58: Three phase integrating focus *(Amendola. L., 2015)*

From my point of view, the most efficient organizations typically follow an integral focus (see Figure 58) that produces savings both immediately and in a permanent manner.

The differential value of this focus resides in going beyond cost savings by creating the bases for growth and innovation after a change in the economic cycle occurs due to a variation in commodities.

Such a focus is made up of three phases:

Phase 1 – Minimize: In this first phase, clearer and more immediate opportunities for budgeting optimization are identified. This stage provides rapid results and maneuverability as it increases trust in the organization in optimizing the costs of CAPEX, the investments in capital goods that create benefits.

Phase 2 - Optimize: Work is carried out on current operations and maintenance (O&M) procedures in a more efficient way, improving asset use (e.g., variable, fixed, instrumentation and electricity) and disincorporating nonessential assets, thereby reducing the cost of O&M in a durable way.

Phase 3 - Redesign: Lastly, structural changes are introduced in a new and more efficient operative O&M model, which provides important improvements in cost of personnel, derived savings from the O&M processes and employment of technologies, people and work processes and new strategies in the direction of competencies and management of change.

When projects are developed, begin by defining the vision objective of the O&M budget, compressing non-discretionary budget items (OPEX) while, at the same time, substantially increasing discretionary investment (CAPEX). The key point is that discretionary spending, far from being reduced, is increased proportionately, as shown in Figure 59.

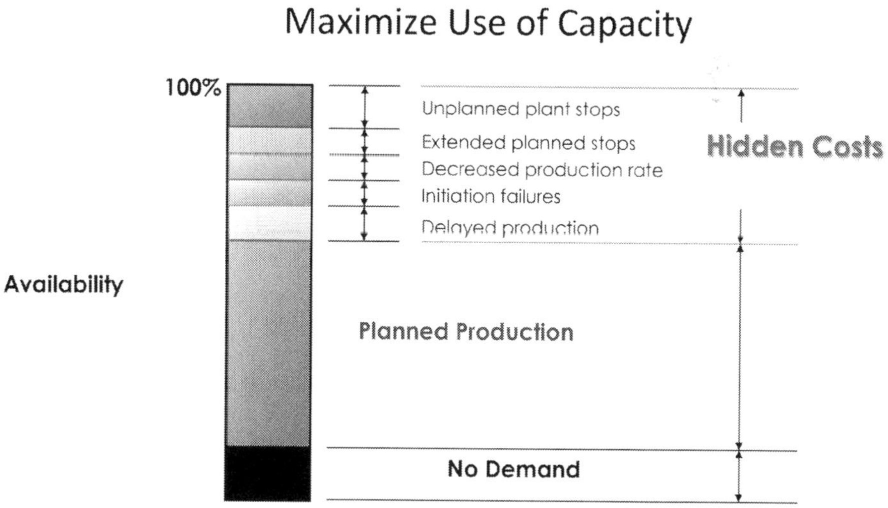

Figure 59: Hidden costs *(Amendola, L., 2010)*

Work is also focused on isolating and eliminating hidden O&M costs. To maximize capacity, focus on such O&M assets (e.g., variable, fixed, instrumentation and electricity) that generate the business value. Afterward, collaborate with those responsible for the finance, human resources, materials, projects, environmental and industrial safety business units to manage demand for O&M services in a more cost-effective way based on a combination of technical and economic indicators.

Without a doubt, this is an ambitious focus, but it assures in a practical way that the optimization of costs and high yields can be reached in the medium and long term range. The benefits of this focus are substantial. Research shows the result of cost optimization is up to three times higher than that reached with a traditional focus.

Indicators for Physical Asset Management

All activities can be measured with parameters that, when focused on decision-making, are signals to monitor management, assuring that activities are run in the correct direction and the results are evaluated by management according to objectives, goals and responsibilities. These signals are known as management indicators.

A management indicator is a measure of the behavior and performance of a process or event in a determined moment. Indicators as a set can provide a broad view of the situation of a process, a business, or the sales of a company. Its magnitude, when compared with some reference level, can be shown as a deviation on which applicable corrective or preventive actions are taken.

Applied in an opportune and updated way, management indicators allow adequate control over a given situation. Their main reason of importance is making it possible to predict and act on the basis of positive or negative tendencies observed with their global performance.

Indicators are also a key feedback mechanism in a process, used for monitoring progress or the execution of a project and strategic plans, among others. And they are even more important if their response time is immediate or very short, allowing for corrective actions to be carried out without delay and in an opportune fashion.

Having a lot of indicators under constant control isn't necessary, rather only the most important ones, the "key ones." The indicators that easily span total performance of a business should receive maximum priority.

The package of indicators can be large or small, depending on the type of business and its specific needs.

In order to work with management indicators, a whole system of indicators must be established that covers the correct understanding of the characteristics and accurate decision-making to maintain, improve and innovate in the process it is in.

Thanks to the development of the total quality management (TQM) philosophy created in the United States and properly applied in Japan, the concept of the management indicator brings success.

In the beginning, its use was oriented more as a control tool of operative processes than as management instruments that support decision-making. Consequently, establishing a system of indicators must involve both the operative processes and the administration of an organization, and must be derived from performance agreements based on the mission and the strategic objectives.

Benefits Derived from Asset Management Indicators

Among the diverse benefits an organization can realize from implementing a system of management indicators are:

Client satisfaction: The identification of company priorities drives yield. As client satisfaction is a company priority, so too will be communicating to personnel and linking strategies with management indicators so employees are driven in that direction and achieve the desired results.

Process monitoring: Continual improvement is only possible if exhaustive follow-up is carried out at each step of the process chain. Measurements are basic tools, not only to detect improvement opportunities, but also to implement actions.

Benchmarking: If an organization wants to improve its processes, a good step is to go beyond its borders and get to know the surroundings in order to learn and implement what is learned. A way of achieving this is through benchmarking to evaluate products, processes and activities, and compare them with those of another company. This practice is easier if one can count on the implementation of reference indicators.

Management of change: An adequate system of measurement allows people to know their contribution to organizational goals and provides results that support the statement that they are doing things well.

Characteristics of management indicators: Management indicators must meet some requisites to be able to support management and achieve their objective. These characteristics can be:

- **Simplicity:** The capacity to define the event that it is meant to be measured in a way that isn't too costly in time and resources.

- **Adequateness:** The ease with which the measurement can fully describe the effect. It must reflect the magnitude of the analyzed fact and show real deviation from the desired level, as well as the standardization of this information.

- **Validity in time:** Defined as the property of being permanent for a desired period.

- **User participation:** The ability to be involved from the design stage. The user must be provided the resources and education necessary for the execution. This is possibly the fundamental ingredient so that employees are motivated around achieving the indicators.

- **Usefulness:** The indicator's ability to always be oriented toward searching for the causes that have led to reaching a particular value and improving them.

- **Opportunity:** The capacity to collect data on time. This requires information to be analyzed opportunely in order to be able to act.

Key Performance Indicators

Key performance indicators (KPIs) are the basis for constructing a big visual display. They are the most effective tool in alerting users about how much and where they are situated with regard to asset management objectives and their strategic plan.

Therefore, it's important to have a clear definition of these elements, which are the basis of the design for your physical asset management strategy.

KPIs are financial or non-financial metrics used to quantify objectives that reflect an organization's yield. Generally found in the strategic asset management plan, these indicators are used for business intelligence to assist or help the current business state to prescribe a line of future action.

The act of monitoring KPIs in real time is known as monitoring business activity. Yield indicators are frequently used to place a value on activities that are difficult to measure, like the benefits of developing leaders, employee commitment, service, or satisfaction.

Earnings Before Interest and Taxes

Earnings before interest and taxes (EBIT) is key to the analysis of company results and shows the benefit obtained in the pure development of the corresponding business. EBIT is the difference between operating revenues and operating expenses for a period, independent of how assets necessary for its development have been financed and applicable taxes on benefits.

It is very useful to compare the evolution of results from one year to the next and between companies in the same sector.

Earnings Before Interest, Taxes, Depreciations and Amortizations

Earnings before interest, taxes, depreciations and amortizations (EBITDA) is obtained by adding amortizations and provisions to EBIT to measure an organization's operating performance. Its use has been generalized over the last years and many analyses show how the organization deals with cash flow or money generated during a period of business. This magnitude must be analyzed with a lot of caution, as it is far from being the true cash flow generated by the business.

Return on Investment

Return on investment (ROI) compares the efficiency of different investment instruments. It is generally expressed as an annual ratio, but also can be expressed as a percentage.

ROI is useful for new businesses to determine whether they are spending their money well, or for existing businesses to determine whether they are making the right new investments.

ROI is a value that measures yield in an investment to evaluate the efficiency of the expenditure you are making or plan to make. A formula exists that gives the calculated value as a function of the investment made and the benefit obtained or the benefit you think you will obtain.

ROI = (Income - Investment) / Investment

The value also can be obtained in this way: **ROI = EBIT ÷ Total Assets (Investment)**

This means you subtract the cost of the investment made from the income you have obtained or plan to obtain from an investment. Then, you divide it by the cost of the investment and the result is the ROI.

For example:

You made an investment of one thousand dollars and obtained three thousand dollars. ROI will be equal to (3000 - 1000) / 1000 = 2

In this example, for each dollar invested, you have obtained two as profit.

In order to know the percentage benefits of your investment, multiply by one hundred. So, with an ROI of two, you are really earning two hundred percent of that invested, having discounted the investment.

ROI is a parameter that is very easy to calculate for knowing how positive an investment has been. The higher the ROI values, the better. If you have a negative ROI, it means you are losing money and if the ROI is very close to zero, it means the investment isn't very attractive. At the time of evaluating your investment, it's a good idea to calculate the ROI, particularly to compare two possible investments. If one investment gets a lower ROI than the other, you should consider investing your money solely in the investment that reports the better proportion.

Additionally, the ROI isolates the benefit of financial management (i.e., financial expenditure) from fiscal policy (i.e., taxes).

ROI can be used for any type of investment. For example, for an asset management replacement (pump P-200), you can calculate this investment with the previous one to figure out the economic return.

Suppose you are making an investment of one thousand dollars on said pump and you obtain twenty-five hundred dollars in sales of your products.

So, the ROI would be (2500 – 1000) / 1000 = 1.5. You would have one hundred and fifty percent from your investment. This value would serve you well when calculating the effectiveness of a campaign, but an analyst would also have to include the personnel, logistics and marketing of the product to earn that twenty-five hundred dollars. Therefore, the real ROI of the campaign would have to take into account your operational costs for obtaining that income. For example, if the cost of logistics was two hundred dollars, the ROI for this case would be (2500 - 200 - 1000) / 1000 = 1.3.

Return on Assets

Return on assets (ROA) is an indicator that measures utilities as a percentage of company assets. ROA represents the profitability of a company with regard to the totality of its assets. This gives you an idea of how efficient the manager (i.e., physical asset director) is in the use of assets to generate income. It's calculated by dividing the company's annual income by its assets to express the ROA as a percentage.

The formula would be:

ROA = Net income = Operational Benefits ÷ Total assets

What Does ROA Help You With?

ROA tells you income generated by invested capital (i.e., assets).

For public companies, it can vary considerably, depending on the industry. Therefore, when using a measure like ROA as a comparative measure, it's better to compare it with previous company values or the ROA of a similar company.

Since company assets are financed by debt and earnings, the ROA ratio gives investors an idea of the company's efficiency in converting the money it has into net income. The higher the ROA, the better because the company is earning more money with less investment.

This investment yield is composed of margin and rotation. The margin is the benefit over sales. The shareholder benefit (i.e., dividend) comes from this same margin.

Rotation is the number of rounds an asset does in a year. The more the asset turns a benefit, the larger the multiplying effect over yield. The quicker it becomes liquid, the higher the asset yield.

You can operate with low profit margins and high rotations, or high margins with low rotations. Benefits also can be obtained on a company's efficiency in asset management.

Example #1:

If a company generates four million dollars as net benefit and has total assets of three hundred thousand, applying the ROA formula would be:

ROA = (4,000,000 / 300,000)

With this strategy, a 13.3 percent ROA is achieved, that is, a profitability of 13.3 percent relative to the assets the company has. In other words, the company uses 13.3 percent of all its assets in the generation of the utility.

Example #2:

If a company has one million dollars of net income and five million dollars in total assets, the ROA is of twenty percent. However, if another company earns the same amount, but has total assets of ten million dollars, it has an ROA of ten percent. Based on this last example, the first company is better in converting its investment into benefits.

The most important task for physical asset directors is to make intelligent decisions in the assignment of resources. Anyone can obtain benefits by placing a ton of money on a problem, but very few administrators are successful in obtaining large profits with little investment.

Return on Equity

Return on equity (ROE) measures utilities as a percentage of employed capital. It measures how much a company has earned compared to shareholder investment. This means the profits the company makes with shareholders' money. This proportion indicates whether the company is investing its money effectively.

ROE also can be used to compare financial actions of competitors in the industry. It is calculated by dividing net income by shareholder equity in the balance.

$$\text{ROE} = \frac{\text{(Operational Profits)}}{\text{(Shareholder Capital)}}$$

$$\text{ROE} = \text{Net benefit} \div \text{Own funds}$$

Example #1:

Energy4U published net benefits this year of five hundred thousand dollars. Suppose in the balance, shareholder equity of Energy4U is two million five hundred thousand dollars.

This would mean:

$500,000 = ROE = 0.20 or 20%

$2,500,000

This means that Energy4U can generate twenty percent over the two million five hundred thousand dollars it has in shareholder equity. The typical ROE in the stock market is between ten and fifteen percent. The return on equity shows how capital in the company is being reinvested. The higher the ROE, the better, but only within the same industry.

ROE does not work when comparing different types of industries since some industries intrinsically have lower ROE than others. For example, pharmaceutical companies can have low ROE because it takes a lot of time and money to develop medication. On the other hand, financial companies can have high ROE because they start to make money immediately.

Example #2:

If a company generates net benefits of four million dollars and has a balance of six hundred thousand, applying the formula: **ROE = (4,000,000 / 600,000).**

The result is an ROE of 6.7 percent, that is, the company has a profitability of 6.7 percent with respect to the balance it possesses. In other words, the company uses 6.7 percent of its earnings in the generation of utilities.

Return on Capital Employed

Return on capital employed (ROCE) is one of the ratios most used by value investors to measure profitability and efficiency of a company.

The formula to calculate ROCE is:

$$ROCE = \frac{EBIT}{Capital\ Employed}$$

Where:

EBIT = Earnings Before Interest and Taxes. (You can find the EBIT in the losses and earnings published annually by companies. You will have to use the annual EBIT or the last twelve months to calculate it correctly.)

Capital Employed = Stockholders' Equity + Debt Liabilities or Assets - Current Liabilities. (To find it, go to the balances published by the company and add or subtract said items. Multiply the result by one hundred and you will have the percentage that indicates the profitability the company obtains over the capital it employs in its current activity.)

The higher the result, the higher the yield and efficiency the company obtains for every dollar of asset capital employed. In this way, you will be able to compare companies on the basis of this ratio and see which is finding better returns.

Replacement Asset Value

Replacement asset value (RAV) consists of the monetary value that would be needed to replace the production capacity of the assets presently in the plant. It includes production equipment or processes, as well as services, support and related assets.

It also includes the replacement value of the buildings and land if they are kept under maintenance expenses. It does not include the value of real estate, only improvements.

RAV, which is synonymous with estimated replacement value (ERV), shouldn't be based on the insured or depreciated value of the assets.

RAV provides the relationship between the total cost of maintenance materials and contracted services (CM) and the cost of replacing assets (CR).

The calculation of RAV is: **RAV = CM/CR**

Data required for the calculation are total current assets, cash and other equivalent liquid assets, short-term investments, net accounts receivable and inventory.

Figure 60 shows the typical RAV percentage, as well as the worst and best in its class

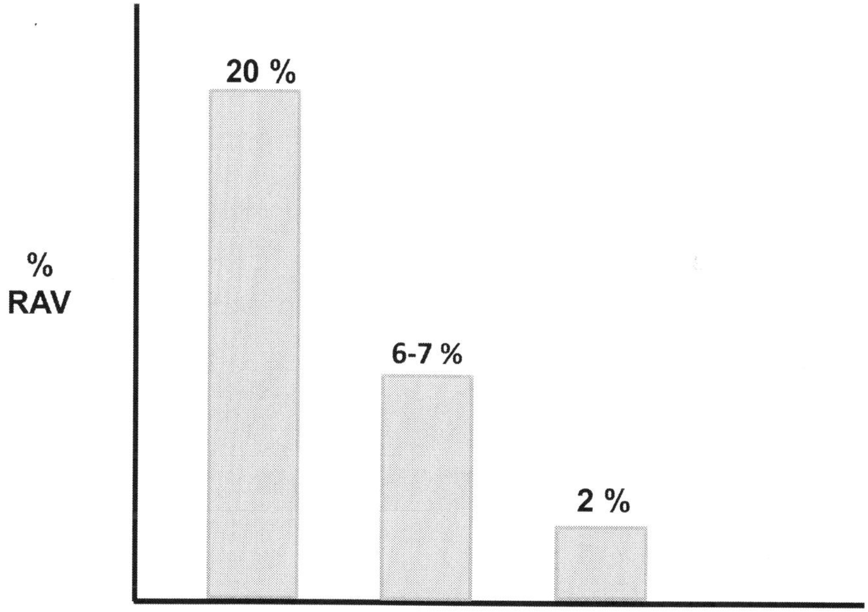

Figure 60: RAV percentage

It's important to remember that minimum maintenance cost is not necessarily the most desirable result. The value of incremental production can be sufficient enough to justify the use of equipment beyond the optimal maintenance point. The key is to know the condition of equipment in plants in order to estimate the best benefit-loss cost of keeping the equipment working or performing maintenance. The real goal is to use the maintenance and personnel budget more efficiently to reduce costs and maintain, or even improve, plant yield.

Maintenance Budget Based on the Replacement Value of Assets

One of the formulas used to obtain a recommended maintenance budget is:

((RCB * MR) + (RCSE * EMR)) * CR = MB

Where:

RCB = Replacement cost of the building or facility. This value can be determined from information and the data the construction costs database provides. This database includes heating, ventilation and air conditioning (HVAC) standards, electrical equipment and plumbing. Replacement costs can be obtained through area estimates.

MR = Maintenance ratio. This number is the percentage of the asset value that must be reinvested to prevent deterioration. The range for standard buildings is one to three percent per annum. The exact quality depends on the use of the facility, the country in which it is located and the type of construction. It's worth mentioning that a two percent maintenance ratio means the whole building would be replaced in the span of fifty years.

RCSE = Replacement cost of production and mobile equipment. It includes production equipment, industrial boilers, mobile equipment, truck fleet, etc. In activity-intense industries, the equipment factor exceeds the cost of facility maintenance by a large margin.

EMR = Equipment maintenance factor. This is equivalent to the maintenance ratio, but for production equipment. The variance of the ratio is between seven and fifteen percent per annum over the RAV. It's worth mentioning that service companies provide full participation contracts and services for parts on electronic equipment for twelve percent of the replacement cost, including benefits.

In the case of several big categories of assets, presenting different factors for the different classes should be considered. For example, a paper mill could have paper machinery in one group and the fleet in another.

CR = Construction ratio. This is the ratio of the time of materials employed for renovations and new constructions relative to the total time invested in all maintenance activities. Construction or installation of new equipment is not a function of maintenance because it isn't required to maintain the asset, however, it is frequently the responsibility of the maintenance department. This includes construction of offices, machinery, new facilities and the creation of a truck fleet.

MB = Maintenance budget. This takes into account work, materials, profit margins and general expenditures, without counting administrative costs.

MB/Sq foot = Maintenance costs per square foot of a building or facility.

MB/Rev = Maintenance budget per revenue dollar.

MB/Out = Maintenance costs per unit output, such as a linear foot of fabric, yards of refuse, patient-days, or ton-miles).

In the article, "Maintenance as a Corporate Strategy," by Andrew Ginder, it is said that world-class manufacturing companies employ maintenance that is around two percent of the RAV.

In some maintenance costs analyses, both types of assets are grouped in the same RAV. Therefore, the two maintenance ratios are also grouped.

Under this focus, calculations will be made to obtain the recommended maintenance budget, such that the formula used would be:

(RAV*MR)*CR=MB

In order to carry out all the calculations, you need the organization to provide the following data:

Calculation of Profitability Indicators	Total current assets
	Total physical assets
	Total debits
	Total income from sales
	Operational costs
Recommended Maintenance Budget	RAV
	MR
	CR

Chef's Recommendations:

It's important to know which parameters will be measured, what the calculated values for the indicators reveal and what measures must be taken in a given case and by whom.

As in the kitchen, we pay attention to the temperature indicators, whether it is well done or not...

Tiger Nut French Toast

Preparation

1. Pour the slightly warm tiger nut beverage in a bowl. (It can be warmed for a few seconds to that it is absorbed by the bread)
2. Take the milk bread or brioche, it's best if it is a day old. Soak in the tiger nut beverage and roll in sugar (ready in a large bowl).
3. Meanwhile, warm a few cubes of butter in a pan (at low heat, as the butter burns almost immediately)
4. When it has melted, we introduce the bread on the pan, until it is golden. You will see how it is left caramelized. Drain the excess fat well and serve with cinnamon powdered on top.
5. It can be accompanied with cinnamon or nougat ice-cream.

Ingredients (4 persons)

- Milk bread / brioche / bread slices
- Butter
- Sugar
- Powdered cinnamon
- Tiger nut sweet beverage
- Cinnamon or nougat ice-cream (optional)

Chef's Comments:

No matter what you've eaten, there will always be room for dessert. It provides a good flavor in your mouth to close a session of good eating. A small plate, without excesses, is tasty, while a lot is tiresome. Let the memory of a little something sweet remain in your palate.

Reflection on Cooking and Asset Management:

Asset management must leave the same taste in your mouth as dessert does.

Digestifs

Valencian Water

Preparation

1. Pour orange juice into a pitcher.
2. Add the cava or champagne
3. Add the vodka and gin
4. Add sugar to taste
5. Refrigerate or add ice to serve cold
6. Add Cointreau, if desired
7. Serve in a wide cocktail glass

Ingredients

- 6 ounces orange juice
- 3 cups cava or champagne
- 3 ounces vodka
- 3 ounces gin
- White sugar
- Ice
- Cointreau, optional

Chef's Comments:

Valencian water is a refreshing beverage and Spain's most emblematic product. The sweet and tasty digestif is the perfect closure to a meal and aids in digestion.

Reflection on Cooking and Asset Management:

The best part of a good meal is digesting, that is, chatting and sharing with friends, loved ones, or if you are alone, well, enjoying your dreams and thoughts.

It is during this time when people talk about diverse topics, try to change the world, etc. In asset management, it can be associated with the analysis of practices, lessons learned and, if you are about to begin an optimization process, talk about and plan the implementation of asset management.

References

1. Amendola, L. "La Confiabilidad desde el Diseño en Proyectos de Mantenimiento." Iberoamérica: 2007; www.mantenimientomundial.com.
2. Amendola, L. and Depool, T. Pilares que Sustentan la Gestión de Activos Físicos "Framework for Sustainability Asset Management", 9th Encuentro Internacional de Mantenimiento de Minas, MAPLA, Chile. 2012.
3. Levin, G. and Skulmoski, G. 'The project management maturity', ESI Horizons, 2(3) (2000) 1–7.
4. Kerzner, H. Strategic Planning for Project Management Using a Project Management Maturity Model. New York: John Wiley & Sons, 2001.
5. Andersen, E.S. and Jessen, S.A. "Project maturity in organizations." International Journal of Project Management, Vol. 21, 2003: 457-461.
6. Demir C. and Kocaba I. "Project Management Maturity Model (PMMM) in Educational Organizations." Science Direct, 2010.
7. Office of Government Commerce. Portfolio, Programme and Project Management Maturity Model. United Kingdom: 2006.
8. Becker, J. and Knackstedt, R. "Developing maturity models for IT management – a procedure model and its applications." Business & Information Systems Engineering, Vol.3, 2009.
9. Kerzner, H. (2006), Project Management maturity Model. John Wiley & Sons, Ins. New York. USA
10. Al-Ahmad, Ahmad. Evaluation of Project Management Maturity: The roles organization influences in the GCC Countries. ESC-Lille University: 2009.
11. Vigil, A.C. CMM y la gerencia de procesos. I Jornada de gerencia de proyectos en TI – ACIS: 2003.
12. Cooke-Davies, T. and Arzymanow, A. "The maturity of project management in different industries: An investigation into variations between project management models." International Journal of Project Management, 2003.
13. Bourne, L. & Tuffley, A. (2007). Comparing Maturity Models: CMMI, OPM3 and P3M3. PMOZ Conference. Practical PM Pty LtCrawford, J. Kent. The Strategic Project Office. New York: Marcel Dekker, 2002.

14. Cleland, David and Ireland, Lewis. Project Manager's Handbook: Applying Best Practices across Global Industries. New York: McGraw-Hill Companies Inc., 2008.
15. (Görog, Mihály y Smith, Nigel J., (2002). "Project Managers for managers"
16. Rodney Turner, J., (1999), "The handbook of project-based project management".
17. Duell, Garry, (June 2000), P.M. Journal.
18. Van Der Merwe, A.P., (1992), P.M. Journal. July 2000.
19. Amendola, L. Integral Management of Physical Assets 3rd Edition (Asset Management) Editorial PMM. 2015
20. Van Horenbeek, A. "Development of a maintenance performance measurement framework using the analytic network process (ANP) for maintenance performance indicator selection." Omega: The International Journal of Management Science, Vol. 42, 2014: pp. 33.
21. Kerzner, H. Project Management: A System Approach to Planning, Scheduling, and Controlling, 8th ed. Hoboken: John Wiley & Sons, 2003.
22. Koontz y O'Donell, 1972. The functions and authority of the manager. Principles of Management: An Analysis of Manageria Functions. McGraw Hill.

Suggested Readings

Amendola, L. Strategies of maintenance management as investment return. 17th European Maintenance Congress, Barcelona, Spain, 2004.

Amendola, L., et al. Methodology for the Implementation of the Project Management Office (PMO). VIII International Congress on Project Engineering, Bilbao, Spain, October, 2004.

Bedford, T. J. and Cooke, R. "Probabilistic risk analysis: foundations and methods." UK: Cambridge University, 2001: 408.

Bridges, Dianne N. and Crawford, J. Kent. How to start up and roll out a project office. Proceedings of the Project Management Institute Annual Seminars & Symposium, Houston, Texas, September 2000.

Bubb, H. "Human Reliability: A Key to improved Quality in Manufacturing." Human Factors and Ergonomics in Manufacturing & Service Industries. Volume 15, 2005: 353-368.

Campbell, J. D. and Reyes-Picknell, J. V. Uptime: Strategies for Excellence in Maintenance Management. New York: Productivity Press Inc., 2006.

Collins, R. Y. and Leathley, B. "Psychological predispositions to errors in safety, reliability and failure analisys." Safety and Reliability, Volume 14, 1995: 6-42.

Crosby, P. B. Quality Is Free: The Art of Making Quality Certain. London: Penguin, 1980.

DeBruin, T., Freeze, R., Kaulkarni, U. and Rosemann, M. Understanding the main phases of developing a maturity assessment model. Association for Information Systems (ACIS) Proceedings, 2005.

Fraser, P. "The use of maturity models/grids as a tool in assessing product development capability." IEEE International Conference on Industrial Engineering and Engineering Management, Vol. 1, 2002: pp. 244.

Galar, D.; Parida, A.; Kumar, U.; Stenstrom, C.; and Berges, L. Maintenance metrics: A hierarchical model of balanced scorecard. Quality and Reliability (ICQR), IEEE International Conference, September 2011.

Grey, Clifford and Larson, Erik. Project Management: The Managerial Process, Fifth Edition. New York: McGraw-Hill Companies Inc., 2011.

Hastings, Nicholas A.J. Physical Asset Management. New York: Springer Publishing, 2010.

Hauck, J. C. Rossa; Caivano, D.; Oivo, M.; Baldassarre, M. T.; and Visaggio, G. Proposing an ISO/IEC 15504-2 Compliant Method for Process Capability/Maturity Models Customization Product-Focused Software Process Improvement. New York: Springer Publishing, 2011.

Hill G.M. "Evolving the Project Management Office: a Competency Continuum." Information Systems Management Journal, 2004: 45-51.

Hollnagel, E. Human Reliability Analysis: Context and Control. Cambridge: Academic Press, 1993.

Hsieh, P. J. "The construction and application of knowledge navigator model (KNM): An evaluation of knowledge management maturity." Expert Systems with Applications Journal, Vol. 36, 2009; 4087.

International Project Management Association (IPMA). The IPMA Delta® Model. http://ipma.ch/certification/certify-organisations/delta-reference-model/

Kaplan, R. and Norton, D. "The Balanced Scorecard measures that drive performance." Harvard Business Review, 1992.

Kaplan, R. and Norton, D. "Having trouble with your strategy? Then Map It." Harvard Business Review, September/October 2000.

Karkukly, Waffa. Managing The PMO Lifecycle: A Step-by-Step Guide to PMO Set-up, Build-out, and Sustainability. Bloomington: Trafford Publishing®: 2012.

Khan, F. I. "Risk-based maintenance (RBM): a quantitative approach for maintenance/inspection scheduling and planning." Journal of Loss Prevention in the Process Industries, Vol. 16, 2003: pp. 561.

Norton. D. "Building A Management System to Implement Your Strategy." Renaissance Solutions, 1996.

Oliva, Rogelio and Watson, Noel, H. "Cross-functional alignment in supply chain planning: A case study of sales and operations planning." Harvard Business School, Working paper 07-001, 2009.

Chemweno Peter; Pintelon, Liliane; and Van Horenbeek, Adriaan. Asset maintenance maturity model as a structured guide to maintenance process maturity. Maintenance Performance Measurement and Management Conference, Lappeenranta, Finland, September 2013.

Porter, M. "What Is strategy." Harvard Business Review, 1996.

Fahrenkrog, Steve, F. Project Management Institute's Organizational Project Management Maturity Model. (OPM3TM). PMI North American Congress, 2003.

Chopra, Sunil and Meindl, Peter. Supply Chain Management: Strategy, Planning, and Operation, Fourth Edition. New York: Pearson, 2010.

Van Horenbeek, A. "Development of a maintenance performance measurement framework using the analytic network process (ANP) for maintenance performance indicator selection." Omega: The International Journal of Management Science, Vol. 42, 2014: pp. 33.

Wendler, R. "The maturity of maturity model research: A systematic mapping study." Information and Software Technology, Vol. 54, 2012: pp.

About the Author

Luis Amendola, Ph.D., is a Founding Partner & CEO Managing Director of PMM Group. He has wide experience in the oil, gas, petrochemical, mining, automotive, energy planning, renewable energy (wind energy) and manufacturing companies and cogeneration.

He is a researcher at the Polytechnic University of Valencia (Spain) in engineering projects and an innovation partner of technical journals and book publishing in Project Management, Asset Management and Maintenance.

He has participated in conferences as a guest speaker and exhibitor of technical papers in local and international events, in companies and universities. He is a member of the editorial staff of publications and professional associations in Europe.

Dr. Amendola is also a business consultant in Europe, Latin America, U.S., Australia, Asia and Africa, with over thirty-five years of experience in the sector. He has two doctorate degrees: Ph.D. in Engineering and Innovation from European University and Ph.D. in Engineering Management from US University.

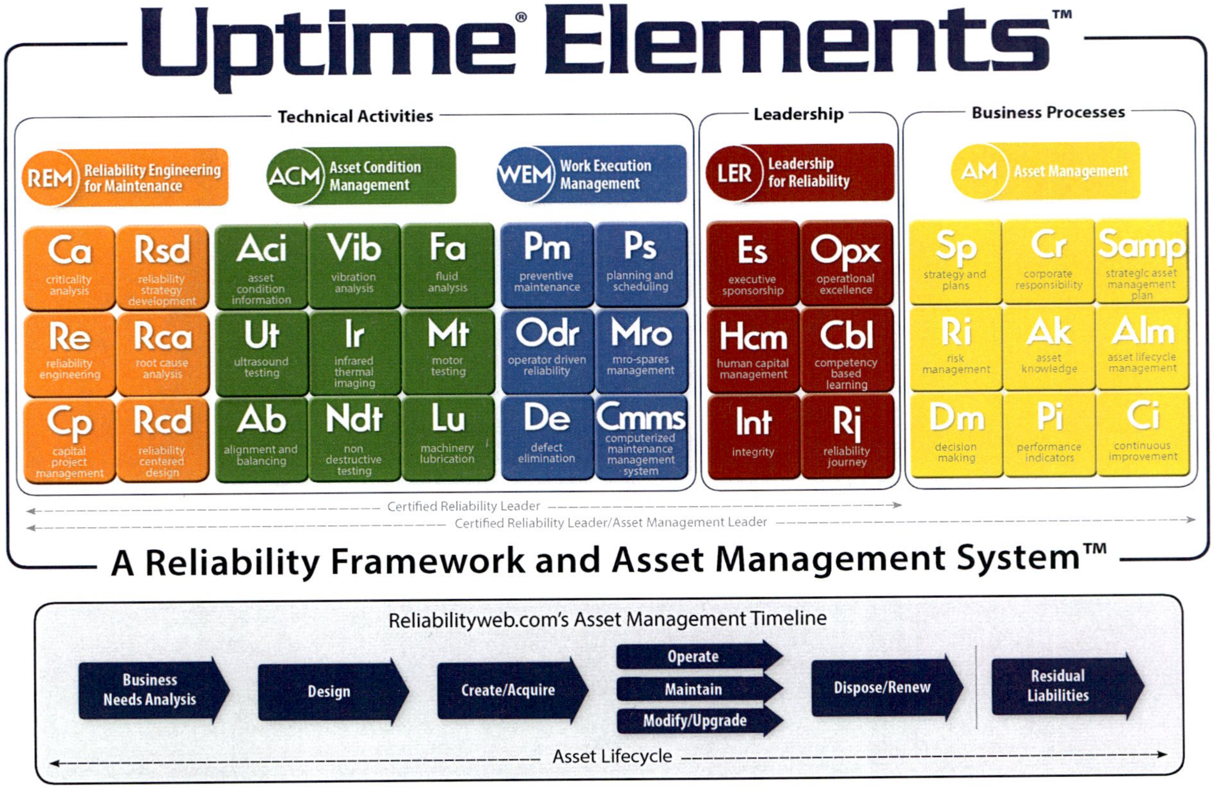

reliabilityweb.com • maintenance.org • reliabilityleadership.com

Reliabilityweb.com® and Uptime® Magazine Mission: To make the people we serve safer and more successful. One way we support this mission is to suggest a reliability system for asset performance management as pictured above. Our use of the Uptime Elements is designed to assist you in categorizing and organizing your own Body of Knowledge (BoK) whether it be through training, articles, books or webinars. Our hope is to make YOU safer and more successful.

About Reliabilityweb.com

Created in 1999, Reliabilityweb.com provides educational information and peer-to-peer networking opportunities that enable safe and effective maintenance reliability and asset management for organizations around the world.

Activities Include:

Reliabilityweb.com® (www.reliabilityweb.com) includes educational articles, tips, video presentations, an industry event calendar and industry news. Updates are available through free email subscriptions and RSS feeds. **Confiabilidad.net** is a mirror site that is available in Spanish at www.confiabilidad.net

Uptime® Magazine (www.uptimemagazine.com) is a bi-monthly magazine launched in 2005 that is highly prized by the maintenance reliability and asset management community. Editions are obtainable in both print and digital.

Reliability Leadership Institute® Conferences and Training Events (www.maintenanceconference.com) offer events that range from unique, focused-training workshops and seminars to small focused conferences to large industry-wide events, including the International Maintenance Conference and The RELIABILITY® Conference.

MRO-Zone Bookstore (www.mro-zone.com) is an online bookstore offering a maintenance reliability and asset management focused library of books, DVDs and CDs published by Reliabilityweb.com.

Association of Asset Management Professionals (www.maintenance.org) is a member organization and online community that encourages professional development and certification and supports information exchange and learning with 50,000+ members worldwide.

A Word About Social Good

Reliabilityweb.com is mission driven to deliver value and social good to the maintenance reliability and asset management communities. *Doing good work and making profit is not inconsistent,* and as a result of Reliabilityweb.com's mission-driven focus, financial stability and success has been the outcome. For over a decade, Reliabilityweb.com's positive contributions and commitment to the maintenance reliability and asset management communities have been unmatched.

Other Causes

Reliabilityweb.com has financially contributed to include industry associations, such as SMRP, AFE, STLE, ASME and ASTM, and community charities, including the Salvation Army, American Red Cross, Wounded Warrior Project, Paralyzed Veterans of America and the Autism Society of America. In addition, we are proud supporters of our U.S. Troops and first responders who protect our freedoms and way of life. That is only possible by being a for-profit company that pays taxes.

I hope you will get involved with and explore the many resources that are available to you through the Reliabilityweb.com network.

Warmest regards,
Terrence O'Hanlon
CEO, Reliabilityweb.com